Savoring Leavenworth

Savoring Leavenworth

Pairing Local Wines with Regional Recipes for
Leavenworth, Peshastin and Cashmere

Compiled by Morgan Fraser

Travel Addict Publishing

SAVORING LEAVENWORTH. Copyright © 2011 by Morgan Fraser. All rights reserved.
No part of this book may be used or reproduced in any manner whatsoever without written permission, except in the case of brief quotations embodied in critical articles and reviews.

For more information, contact:

Travel Addict Publishing
P.O. Box 3743
Wenatchee, WA 98807-3743
morgan@savoringchelan.com

SavoringLeavenworth.com

Back cover photo by Richard Uhlhorn.
Cover art by Kerry Siderius.
Cover design by Kasey Koski.

ISBN 978-0-9829566-1-8

Printed in the United States of America by InstantPublisher.com

LEAVENWORTH   **WASHINGTON**

A portion of the proceeds from the sale of this book go to the Community Cupboard, a program of Upper Valley M.E.N.D. (Meeting Each Need with Dignity) in Leavenworth.

M.E.N.D operates through a dedicated community of volunteers and staff, providing emergency family assistance and food bank services, affordable housing opportunities, free health care services, and support for adults with developmental disabilities.

In addition to providing food bank services to more than 200 local families each month, the Community Cupboard provides emergency family assistance, including rental, utility, fuel and transportation assistance and emergency shelter. They also run a local thrift store.

"M.E.N.D. engages our community in transforming lives through actions grounded in faith, hope and love."

For more information and to donate to M.E.N.D., go to uvmend.org.

TABLE OF CONTENTS

Foreword 1
Introduction by Joanne Saliby, *Living Well* Blog Author 2
Wineries 3

Appetizers 21
- Apple Pecan Brie 23
- Beecher Hill Roasted Grapes 24
- Gorgonzola Balsamic Fruit Plate 26
- Mushroom, Tomme & Roasted Tomato Crostini 27
- Perfectly Pesto Cheesecake 29
- Salsa Verde 31
- Sweet & Savory Pineapple Salsa 32
- Walnut Crusted Brie with Apple Cherry Chutney 33

Soups and Salads 35
- Bleu Cheese Pear Salad 37
- Beet Salad 38
- Chorizo Yam Bisque 40
- Gazpacho Blanco 41
- Grilled Ahi Tuna Salad 42
- Gumbo 43
- Tarragon and Crab Stuffed Tomatoes 44

Entrees 45
- Apple Sweet Potato Roast Pork 47
- Artist's Vacation Greek Lamb 48
- Balsamic Glazed Salmon 49
- Butternut Squash Ravioli with Sage Butter 50
- Creamy Smoked Salmon & Asparagus 53
- Dave's Mac & Cheese 54
- Feta Mint Lamb Burgers 55
- Flank Steak Portabella Sandwiches 56
- Gnocchi with Roasted Tomato Red Pepper Sauce 57
- Grilled Lamb Burgers in Red Wine 60
- Hambleton Hominy Casserole 61
- Herb's Sweet & Tangy Salmon Sauce 62
- Lemon Crab Linguini 65

Table of contents continues on following page

Table of Contents (Continued)

Entrees (continued)
- Lobster Mac & Cheese 66
- Mediterranean Rack of Lamb 67
- Mole de Oaxaca 68
- Mushroom Artichoke Chicken 71
- Mushroom Risotto 72
- Red Wine Cherry Pork 73
- Roast Pork Loin with Bartlett Pear Sauce 75
- Saffron Quail 76
- Salmon in Balsamic Blackberry Wine Sauce 78
- Scalloped Oysters 79
- Shrimp Etouffee 80
- Spaghetti with Merlot Tomato Sauce 81
- Sweet & Spicy Black Beans 82
- Thai Cashew Chicken 83
- Thai Coconut Bouillabaisse 84
- Tuscan Cabbage and Mushrooms 86

Desserts 87
- Audrey's Apple Pie 89
- Audrey's Pie Crust 90
- Caramel Sauce with Apple Wine 91
- Grandma Judy's Sour Cream Pear Pie 92
- La Toscana Apple Coffee Cake 93
- Mango Raspberry Cobbler 94
- Raspberry Cheesecake Sauce 95
- Orchard Pear Tart 96
- Salted Caramel Chocolate Mousse Cheesecake 99
- Wine Poached Pear Sorbet 102
- Wine Soaked Cherries and Pears Over Pound Cake 103

Contributors 105
Index 111
Washington Fruit Harvest Dates 118
Acknowledgements 119
About the Author 120

Foreword

Welcome to *Savoring Leavenworth*, a cookbook that pairs Leavenworth, Peshastin and Cashmere wines with recipes from local restaurants and wineries.

This book is meant to offer an insider's view of the Leavenworth area. Not only will you find recipes and wine pairings from area experts, you will also discover sources for fresh, high quality produce and products.

This cookbook was created for readers drawn to the area for its beauty, climate, food and wines. The chefs, winemakers, winery owners, artists and photographers who contributed to *Savoring Leavenworth* shared their love of the area through their suggestions and recipes, knowing that Leavenworth fans would be as excited to receive the information as they were to provide it.

Leavenworth is not simply a Bavarian village in Central Washington. It is also a hub for enjoying local wines, fresh fruit, fresh fish, locally grown produce, a small-town feel, and the beauty of a mountain setting in any season.

How To Use This Book

I recommend you read through a recipe completely before beginning to cook, in order to get a feel for the timing and difficulty level. I also advise having all the ingredients chopped and set out as listed in the recipe before starting.

The wine pairings are suggestions to give you an idea of what would go well with the dishes. An index in the back of the book allows you to cross-reference which recipes are listed with your favorite wines. However, they are by no means the only wines that complement the dishes. Pairing depends largely on personal taste, and while one person may completely agree with a wine pairing suggestion, another may prefer something else entirely. The Leavenworth area offers wines for every palate: With a little bit of experimentation, you can find a recipe and a wine that will fit any occasion.

Savoring Leavenworth has something for everyone. The recipes appeal to a wide range of personal tastes and feature varying levels of difficulty, preparation and cook time. To try something new or find a new twist on an old favorite, simply explore the recipes, pictures and commentary from the people who know the area's food and wine best.

If the recipe contributor is a winery owner, you will be directed to their winery page at the beginning of the book. Otherwise, you will find the contributor's information in the contributor's section at the back.

In many cases, the contributors included recommendations on where to find ingredients locally. If you are not in the Leavenworth area, you can usually find the item – or a comparable product – at your local grocery store.

Enjoy!

Morgan Fraser, author, *Savoring Chelan* and *Savoring Leavenworth*

Introduction

North Central Washington is the late bloomer as a wine region in the state, but isn't it true that late blooms often outshine even the best that summer has to offer?

I've been fortunate in having been here almost since the beginning. I visited Warren and Julie Moyles before they'd excavated the cellar and hung out their sign at La Toscana. I live on the north face of the hills, across the creek from Eagle Creek Winery's south-facing vineyards, and from my living room window watched Ed Rutledge hand build his home and then the winery building, and saw the plantings of the grapes in the Eagle Creek estate vineyards. My granddaughter graduated with Rob Newsom's daughter, and I knew the wines of Boudreaux Cellars when they were built in the tiny garage just outside the main house. I still thank Rob and Tamara for giving me my first taste of an Andrew Will wine in the cellar of their main house. Now Rob and others make their own world class wines.

My early involvement in the explosion of wine industry activity in our area is the main reason I was interested to learn that Morgan was working on a second volume about wineries in and near Leavenworth. Having enjoyed *Savoring Chelan*, I was happy to see that she had similar goals for wines in the Leavenworth community, so I volunteered to help her in any small way she thought I might contribute to the book.

Each year, Leavenworth attracts many thousands of visitors who come for the charm of the Bavarian town with its Oktoberfest, Christmas Lighting, outdoor activities, theater and music – and now, for the wine. Many local chefs use local products whenever possible to prepare dishes complementary to the local wines. These same chefs, along with winemakers and winery owners, have joined local residents in offering recipes to pair with these wines. Now, with *Savoring Leavenworth*, you can prepare many of these dishes at home and enjoy them with the wines you take home with you. You might find you prefer pairing some recipes with our local beers, while some, especially the delicious desserts, can stand alone or be accompanied by tea or coffee.

I've read all the recipes submitted by those participating in Morgan's latest effort and suggested most of the wine pairings for their dishes. I am happy to say I've even contributed a few recipes myself. I hope you find the volume both enjoyable and practical.

Joanne Saliby
Author, Wenatchee World *Living Well* Blog

Wineries and Tasting Rooms

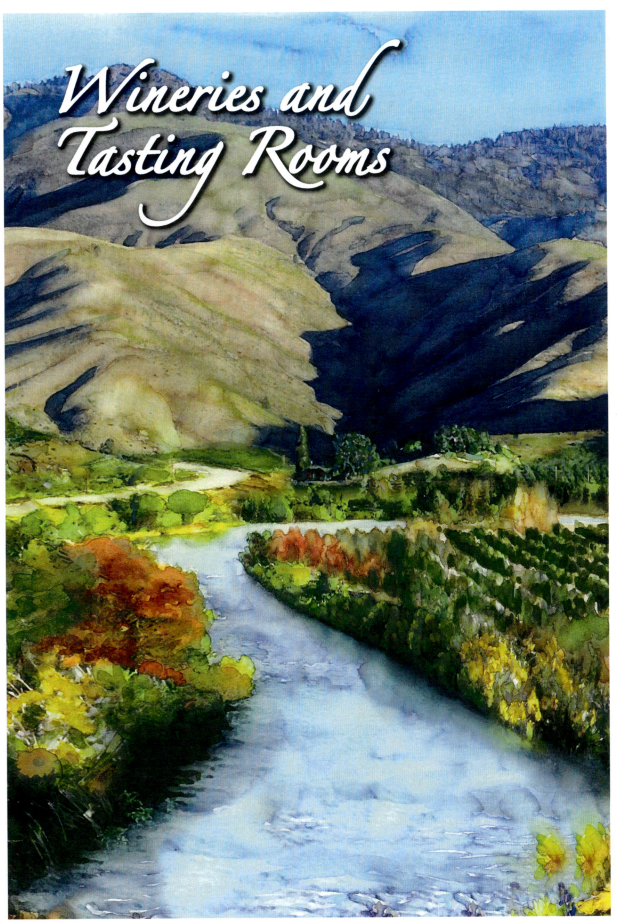

"Wenatchee River Through the Vineyard" by Kerry Siderius

Wineries and Tasting Rooms

"Grapes with Yellow Leaf" by Kerry Siderius

'37 Cellars

Left: The view of the Enchantments from the '37 Cellars tasting room and winery.

Below: Chuck Egner "punching down" or breaking up the cap on top of the fermenting juice. Punching down rehydrates the skins that float to the top and gets oxygen to the yeast.

Photos by Reed Carlson

'37 Cellars was created in September 2005 with the crush of the winery's very first fruit, Cabernet Sauvignon from the Columbia Valley. Owners Chuck and Candace Egner and Frank and Harriett Dechaine are in-laws, and have been friends for more than 30 years. Their intention was to make fine, handcrafted wine for their own enjoyment. If others liked it, so much the better.

This year marks the Egner's and Dechaine's seventh crush. While most of '37 Cellars wine is Cabernet Sauvignon, they also craft Merlot, Chardonnay, and the occasional Bordeaux-style blend. Their fruit is grown in some of the most prestigious old-vine vineyards in the state of Washington, including Pepper Bridge, Bacchus and Dionysus of Sagemoor Farms, Seven Hills West and Gamache. '37 Cellar's fruit-forward wines have great nose, color and texture. Visitors enjoy wine tasting with unmatched views of the Cascade Mountains, and perhaps an impromptu song played on one of the 1937 Martin D 18 guitars, for which the winery is named.

'37 Cellars
8210 Dempsey Rd.
Leavenworth, WA
509.548.8663
37cellars.com

Bella Terrazza Vineyards

Photo by Reed Carlson

Bella Terrazza garden tasting room in Wenatchee.

Bella Terrazza Vineyards is situated on an ideal south-facing slope above the Wenatchee River. The winery is named for its location – *bella terrazza* means "beautiful terrace" in Italian.

The owners take pride in their artisan-style wines, produced from grapes grown on vines that have been carefully trained for years. Almost every aspect of grape growing – from the training and pruning to harvest – is done by hand. Many of the vines are grown on hand-cut terraces, one of the few estate wineries in Washington that does this. Reminiscent of "Old-World" European vineyards, Bella Terrazza produces a number of varieties in that artisan style, such as Riesling, Gewürztraminer, Lemberger, Cabernet Franc, Sangiovese, Syrah, Muscat, Barbera, Pinot Gris and Chardonnay.

Visit Bella Terrazza Vineyard's outdoor covered tasting room, as well as their sister business, Sleepy Hollow Nursery. Enjoy U-pick blueberries and have a picnic on the lawn during the summer. They also have a year-round tasting room in Leavenworth, in the heart of downtown.

Bella Terrazza Leavenworth Tasting Room
837 Front St., Ste. A
Leavenworth, WA

Bella Terrazza Winery & Garden Tasting Room
1260 Lower Sunnyslope Rd.
Wenatchee, WA

509.662.9141
bellaterrazzavineyards.com

Boudreaux Cellars

Photo by Richard Uhlhorn

Boudreaux Cellars owner and winemaker Rob Newsom, holding a dish of Saffron Quail. See the recipe on page 76.

Nestled in the Cascade Mountains near Leavenworth and totally off the power grid, Boudreaux Cellars is a small winery that produces beautiful wines that adore food.

Winemaker Rob Newsom, a Louisiana native with a sly sense of humor, brought his Southern background with him. Although he's been in Washington for nearly 20 years, he named the winery after an infamous Cajun legend: Boudreaux is a man who fishes with dynamite and is always getting into mischief.

In 2007, Rob and Boudreaux Cellars were awarded "Best New Winemaker" and "Best New Winery" by Seattle Magazine. Rob's focus on smooth, deeply complex reds produces ultra-premium wines, including Merlot, Syrah, Cabernet Sauvignon, Reserve Cabernet and "Frangio," half Sangiovese and half Cabernet Franc. He also offers an unfiltered Chardonnay and a Riesling from Gamache Vineyard.

Rob's handcrafted wines are made with fruit sourced from some of the most coveted vineyards in the state. Since his winery is off the power grid, Rob stores his barrels in an underground cellar for aging, a process that maintains constant temperatures naturally but takes 2-3 years to complete, longer than average. Rob says the natural aging process has been a large part of making his wine a success.

Boudreaux Cellars
4551 Icicle Creek Rd.
Leavenworth, WA
509.548.5858
boudreauxcellars.com

Photo by Richard Uhlhorn

Wineries & Tasting Rooms

Cascadia Winery

The wine spark was lit for Alan Yanagimachi after dining with Robert Mondavi in 1983. Buoyed by Mondavi's suggestion to pursue an education in winemaking, Alan earned a degree in Fermentation Science/Enology from the University of California Davis.

From there, Alan spent more than a decade working in wineries throughout Washington and California. He also worked for 18 months in the former Soviet Republic of Georgia, one of the oldest wine-making regions in the world. This brought Alan the joy of understanding the value of wine as an essential element of lifestyle.

Photo courtesy Cascadia Winery
Wall mural by Gibbs Graphics

Cascadia Winery tasting room in Peshastin.

Cascadia Winery opened in 2006 and represents Alan's desire to develop wines that people can enjoy as part of their daily lives. His number one seller is Cascadia Apple Wine, made completely of Golden Delicious and Gala apples from Central Washington. Alan's apple wine accounts for 60 percent of his bottled wine sales. He also creates a Sakura Dessert wine, the only one of its kind in Washington State. The Sakura – or "cherry blossom" – wine is a mixture of Merlot and 100 percent dark cherry juice; it is a favorite amongst area chefs and one of Cascadia's most popular wines. Alan is also known for his Roussanne and Merlot.

Cascadia Winery
10090 Main St., Ste F
Peshastin, WA
509.548.7900
cascadiawinery.com

CRAYELLE CELLARS

Photos by Richard Uhlhorn

Winery co-owner Danielle Mitrakul serves wine to guests at the Crayelle Cellars tasting room in Cashmere.

Crayelle Cellars owners Craig and Danielle Mitrakul released their first vintage of wines in November 2009. Even though their label is new, Craig is not a newcomer to the wine industry: he has nearly 15 years of winemaking experience spanning four wine regions at home and abroad. He's worked in Australia, the Finger Lakes of New York, Oregon's Willamette Valley and has extensive experience in the Washington wine industry, including Chateau Ste. Michelle, Three Rivers, Ryan Patrick and Saint Laurent wineries. Prior to entering the wine industry, Craig earned a bachelor's Degree from Rutgers University and a master's degree in Food Science with an emphasis in Enology from Cornell University. His extensive training and experience are the driving force behind Crayelle Cellars.

Craig and Danielle are both passionate about Syrah and dry Riesling, which make up the vast majority of their production. The grapes are sourced from vineyards in the Ancient Lakes area in Quincy, WA. The grapes grown in this area are ideal for the style of wines they craft: wines that pair well with food and are aromatic with balanced acidity.

Crayelle Cellars
207A Mission Ave.
Cashmere, WA
509.393.1996
crayellecellars.com

WINERIES & TASTING ROOMS

Eagle Creek Winery & d'Vinery Tasting Room

When Ed Rutledge began making wines for his friends and family in his home, he never dreamed he would have a tasting room on his property, much less a second location. Eagle Creek Winery has been a family owned and operated winery since 2000, making it the oldest winery in Leavenworth. It is the home of Ed and Patricia Rutledge, their winery, tasting room and cottage. The Rutledges take pride in producing only the highest quality premium wines at affordable prices. Ed personally selects grapes from his own vineyard and other exceptional vineyards in Washington's Columbia Valley to make Eagle Creek's wines.

Visit the Eagle Creek Winery May through October to taste extraordinary wines, peruse their custom-made wine cellar and sip a glass of wine on their shaded patio overlooking the vineyard. You can also enjoy the same wines year round in downtown Leavenworth at their satellite tasting room, d'Vinery.

Photo by Richard Uhlhorn

Photo by Richard Uhlhorn

Eagle Creek Winery
10037 Eagle Creek Rd.
Leavenworth, WA
509.548.7668
eaglecreekwinery.com

d'Vinery Tasting Room
617 Front St., #4A,
Leavenworth, WA
509.548.7059
dvinery.com

Horan Estates Winery & Tasting Room

Photo by Richard Uhlhorn

Horan Estates owners, left to right: Dennis and Beth Dobbs, Diana and Doug McDougall.

In 2000, Doug McDougall planted an organic apple orchard on the south slope of the Frenchman Hills near Royal City, Washington. He included two acres of Syrah wine grapes on land near his orchard, just to see how they would grow.

In 2002, Doug sold the first grape harvest to a well-known winemaker from the Tri-Cities area. When the winemaker praised the high quality of the grapes he received, Doug, his wife Diana and friends Ross and Kelly Riedinger started a small winery in Wenatchee Heights using Doug's grapes from Royal City. In the fall of 2010, Doug's cousin, Beth Dobbs, joined the McDougalls to help market Horan Estates award-winning wines to local wine shops and restaurants. In the spring of 2011, Beth and her husband Dennis became partners in the winery after the Riedingers decided to move on to other ventures.

Since its first vintage in 2003, Horan Estates has concentrated on crafting three red wines. CWM Syrah is named after the McDougalls' only son, Corey Wayne McDougall, who was killed in a tragic snowmobiling accident in December 2003. The HVH Red Blend is dedicated to Doug and Beth's grandmother, Helen VanDivort Horan, who passed away peacefully in January 2004 at the age of 100. The third is the Cabernet Sauvignon, produced from the five clones planted in the expanded eight-acre vineyard near Royal City. A new wine production facility was constructed next door to the current tasting room in Cashmere. The McDougalls and Dobbs began crushing operations at this location in the fall of 2011.

Horan Estates Tasting Room
207 Mission Ave., Ste. D
Cashmere, WA

Horan Estates Winery
206 Mission Ave.
Cashmere, WA

509.860.0662 or 509.679.8705
horanestateswinery.com

Icicle Ridge Winery & Tasting Room

Photo courtesy Icicle Ridge Winery

Icicle Ridge Winery by night.

    Located in the foothills of the Cascade Mountains near Leavenworth, Icicle Ridge Winery is aptly named for its amazing views of Icicle Ridge. Founder Lou Wagoner and winemaker Don Wood produce hand-crafted, award-winning wines that will delight you. "Welcome Home to Icicle Ridge" is what you will most likely be greeted with as you enter the spectacular log home tasting room in Peshastin. It makes sense, as you are entering the 5,000 square foot *home* of Louie and Judy Wagoner. In 1990, Lou and Judy Wagoner began building the log home on the North Road of Peshastin, overlooking Icicle Ridge Mountain. In 2000, American pear prices were drastically dropping, so Lou began planting grapes. By 2002, the log home's doors were open to the public to taste wine bottled by the Wagoners.

    Many of Icicle Ridge's wines have been praised in numerous publications and contests, but the biggest awards come straight off the wine-stained lips of their cherished guests. Whether it's the estate grown ice wines, specialty fruit wines or the well-known classic varietals, there is a wine at Icicle Ridge for everyone.

Icicle Ridge Winery
8977 North Rd.
Peshastin, WA
509.548.7019

Icicle Ridge Tasting Room
821 Front St., Ste. B
Leavenworth, WA
509.548.6156

icicleridgewinery.com

La Toscana Winery

Photo by Reed Carlson

La Toscana owner and winemaker Warren Moyles with Smokey, the winery mascot.

"La Toscana" (Italian for "Tuscany") Winery grew from a longstanding love affair with the Tuscan region in Italy where wine, food and hospitality reign supreme.

After spending more than 20 years abroad as teachers in Department of Defense schools – including several years in northern Italy – Warren and Julie Moyles came home to North Central Washington. They were inspired to recreate some of the ambience they had enjoyed while living overseas. On a small piece of land just east of Leavenworth, they planted a half-acre of wine grapes as an experimental hobby. By the late '90s, they were producing wine.

Local folks were skeptical, but the grapes flourished, and by early 2000, Warren had obtained a license and ramped up production to 400 cases a year in a "Mom and Pop" style operation, the first of its kind in the region.

Aiming to craft mostly rustic Italian blends, La Toscana began specializing in mellow mélanges of Sangiovese, Cabernet Sauvignon, Cabernet Franc, Merlot and Lemberger using grapes from the Red Mountain and Mattawa regions. A signature characteristic began to emerge in La Toscana reds: soft tannins, layered flavors, a long finish. Their loyal customer base continued to build.

As other wineries sprouted rapidly throughout the valley, La Toscana was soon surpassed in size and scope, but retained its rural flavor and low-volume output. The sharing of labor and laughter with their friends reminded the Moyles of happy years in Europe and remain among the most cherished memories of their winemaking years.

La Toscana Winery and Guest Suite
9020 Foster Rd.
Cashmere, WA
509.548.5448
latoscanawinery.com
Tastings by appointment only

Pasek Cellars/Willow Crest Tasting Room

In August 2004 a partnership was formed between Pasek Cellars and Willow Crest Winery when they opened a tasting room in Leavenworth. The tasting room features Pasek fruit wines and Willow Crest's European-style dry red and white wines.

Photo courtesy Pasek Cellars/Willow Crest Tasting Room

The Pasek Cellars/Willow Crest Tasting Room in Leavenworth.

Gene and Kathy Pasek started Pasek Cellars in 1995 in Mt. Vernon. From the start they had a tiger by the tail. Gene's fruit wines had achieved incredible popularity. The winery's production grew steadily, but still at a rate where demand often outstripped their ability to produce.

David Minick, a longtime grape grower in the Yakima Valley, founded Willow Crest Winery in 1995. The Minick family first planted wine grapes on their Roza farm, North of Prosser, in 1982. David wanted to take the love he had for raising grapes to the next level by making premium wine out of a small portion of the family vineyard. By having the control from vine to wine, David can monitor crop load, canopy size, sun exposure, and the balance of fruit and sugar at harvest time.

Pasek Cellars/Willow Crest
Tasting Room
939 Front St., Ste. B
Leavenworth, WA
509.548.5166
willowcrestwinery.com
pasekcellars.com

Ryan Patrick Vineyards

Photo by Richard Uhlhorn

Toni Lawrence serves wine to visitors at the Ryan Patrick tasting room in Leavenworth.

Terry Flanagan grew up near Quincy, Washington, and returned there in 1996 after retiring from his corporate career. He planted the vineyards on land that has been in his family for three generations. The vineyards produce Merlot, Cabernet Sauvignon, Cabernet Franc and award-winning Chardonnay. Ryan Patrick Vineyards is the creation of Terry and Vivian Flanagan and named for their two sons, Ryan and Patrick.

Ryan Flanagan, a Gonzaga University graduate, began supervising the family vineyards after gaining experience at Chateau Ste. Michele in Woodinville, and currently manages Evergreen Vineyards as well as the Ryan Patrick Estate Vineyards.

Patrick Flanagan, who died in 2004 in a car accident, was an up-and-coming winemaker in his own right; in 2006, his wines won some of the highest Wine Spectator scores the Flanagans received.

Winemaking has been conducted under the supervision of Craig Mitrakul. Craig's extensive education and his worldwide winemaking experiences inspired Wine Press Northwest to name him "one of the up and coming winemaking stars in Washington" in 2003. Craig has lived up to this accolade by creating some of Washington's finest wines.

The Flanagan's goal was always to create top-quality grapes that would in turn create high quality wines.

"From the beginning, our goal has been to produce limited quantities of reserve quality wines at affordable prices," Terry Flanagan said. "Quality – not quantity – has always been our main priority."

Ryan Patrick Vineyards Tasting Room
636 Front Street
Leavenworth, WA
509.888.2236
ryanpatrickvineyards.com

Silvara Vineyards

Silvara Vineyards was founded in 2008 by Gary Seidler, who received his oncology credentials from UC Davis, and Cindy Rarick, a 25-year professional golfer.

Photos by Marissa Maharaj

The Silvara tasting room is perched on a hill above Highway 2 between Leavenworth and Peshastin.

The winery specializes in both red and white Bordeaux, Italian, and German style wines. The tasting room is poised on a gentle hillside overlooking the Wenatchee River. It is surrounded by wildflower-carpeted hillsides, pear orchards, and the majestic wooded peaks of the Cascade Mountains. The five-acre estate boasts a magnificent 4,000 square foot tasting room with a towering scissor-truss roof frame, expansive windows, and stone fireplaces warming the front great room. It is equipped with an outdoor wood fired pizza oven and a full kitchen for banquets. They host everything from wine dinners to serving light fare to those who drop in to the tasting room looking to relax.

Silvara's current wines include Malbec, Chardonnay, Riesling, Merlot, Cabernet Sauvignon, Syrah, Pinot Grigio, and their 60/40 blend: 60 percent Merlot, 40 percent Cabernet Sauvignon.

Silvara Vineyards
77 Stage Rd.
Leavenworth, WA
509.548.1000
silvarawine.com

Stemilt Creek Winery

Photo by Richard Uhlhorn

The Stemilt Creek tasting room in Leavenworth.

At the turn of the 20th century, the Mathison family planted their first fruit trees atop their Stemilt Hill homestead, igniting a tradition that has thrived for five generations. Today, world-class fruit growers Kyle and Jan Mathison apply that wisdom and passion as vintners, paying special attention to every stage of the growing process, from the soil to the lips.

The creation of Stemilt Creek Wine begins with a uniquely crafted organic compost, tilled on location at Stemilt Hill. Careful of each ingredient, this compost boasts a balanced acidity specifically designed for a grapevine's optimal growth.

Next, the grapes are nourished, picked, crushed and processed in barrels on site. Actively involved in each step of this process, a dedicated team celebrates every stage of the life of the grape and takes joy in its journey at Stemilt Hill. The Stemilt heritage in the fruit industry offers yet another benefit to this process: all wine is produced in a climate-controlled warehouse. This high level of direction ensures the best possible environment for winemaking.

All the Stemilt Creek red wines are created from their estate vineyards, including Cabernet Sauvignon, Merlot, Syrah, Cabernet Franc and the Stemilt Hill Red. They also offer Sweet Adelaide, a white blend of Riesling, Gewürztraminer and Chardonnay sourced from the Columbia Valley.

Leavenworth Tasting Room
617 Front St., Ste. 4A
Leavenworth, WA
509.888.5357

Wenatchee Tasting Room
110 N. Wenatchee Ave.
Wenatchee, WA
509.665.3485

stemiltcreekwinery.com

Swakane Winery & Tasting Room

Swakane Winery is a boutique winery overlooking the mighty Columbia River. They produce just 500 cases a year of award-winning whites, reds and berry wines.

Donna and Mike Franks began their journey in 2000 making wine at home for themselves. Mike's love for winemaking continued to grow, and soon he was in school every weekend working on his degree in Enology. "The Art of Wine Making" taught him everything that goes into a glass of wine, from the soil the grapes are grown in to the bottles the wine is later poured from, and every detail in between.

Photo by Richard Uhlhorn

The Swakane Winery tasting room in Leavenworth.

Mike handcrafts all of Swakane's wine on site from both Swakane Estate grapes and grapes from other premium vineyards throughout Washington State. They produce small lots of each varietal, allowing Mike to pay special attention to detail and earning him awards for his Merlot, Cabernet Sauvignon and Estate Late Harvest Riesling. Swakane also produces Estate Sauvignon Blanc, Estate Cabernet Franc, Estate Rosé of Cabernet Franc, Rocky Reach Red blend, and Willapa Wild Blackberry Dessert Wine, using 100 percent wild blackberries from Willapa Bay in Southwest Washington.

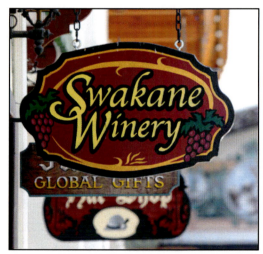

Photo by Richard Uhlhorn

**Swakane Winery
Tasting Room & Bistro**
725 Front St.
Leavenworth, WA
509.888.7225

Swakane Winery & Tasting Room
(6 miles north of Wenatchee)
7980 State Hwy. 97A,
Wenatchee, WA
509.662.1928

swakanewinery.com

Waterville Winery Tasting Room

Photo by Richard Uhlhorn

Waterville Winery owner Lisa Wareham tasting her wares.

In 1992, Matt and Lisa Wareham began dreaming about having a good time making great wine and selling it at affordable prices. In 2006, they were officially licensed to make wine out of their garage in Waterville, Washington, a classic small town east of the Columbia River above Orondo, and the highest in the state, at 2,750 feet elevation. They opened their tasting room in Cashmere's Mission District in June 2010.

Their label is a self-portrait of Matt, the winemaker, under a sign that says, "Vin du Garagiste," (Wine of the Garage Winemaker), drawn using dry-erase marker.

Their garage enterprise produces Chardonnay and Cabernet Sauvignon, both from vineyards near Quincy, Washington and the Gorge Amphitheater. Lisa and Matt think the historic 2006 musical lineup at the Gorge had a large impact on the outcome of their 2006 Cabernet Sauvignon; the terroir combined the best of Columbia River soil with weekly sound showers. Why wouldn't the grapes be anything but extremely happy, rocking out to Death Cab, Dave Matthews, NIN, Bouncing Souls and Pearl Jam?

Their Viognier, Gewürztraminer, Cabernet Franc and Riesling are grown by Cat's Hollow Vineyard in Wenatchee.

Waterville Winery also makes the only wine-based wine cooler on the market: it is a Chardonnay wine, blended with fruit juices and sold in 12-ounce bottles.

Waterville Winery Tasting Room
207 Mission Ave.
Cashmere, WA
509.630.8851
watervillewinery.com

Wedge Mountain Winery

An exquisite bottle of wine, a memory for all time.

This is what Charlie and Mary Ann McKee hope that you will take away from Wedge Mountain Winery. The romance and mystique of wine country are alive and well at Wedge Mountain, whether you are tasting wine in the underground cave, behind the thick walls of the straw bale building, or outdoors in an "orchard garden." Although apple and pear trees dot the landscape before you, it is only a short walk from the tasting room to the Stony Hill "Vineyard-by-the-River."

Photo by Reed Carlson

Wedge Mountain Winery owners Charlie and Mary Ann McKee at their tasting room and winery in Peshastin.

Charlie is devoted to his winemaking, and will tell you that each vintage has its own unique character. As the seasons pass, the vineyard changes and the grapes respond in myriad ways to subtle shifts in climate and soils, expressing their terroir. Charlie's task is to capture these magical nuances in each new vintage of the wine, and to present to you the best of the best, whether it's his Pinot Grigio, Dry Riesling, Chardonnay, Cabernet Franc, Cabernet Sauvignon, Merlot, Trios Chevaux Rouges (red blend), Lemberger or his Roses and Rubies dessert wine.

Wedge Mountain Winery
9534 Saunders Road
Peshastin, WA
509.548.7068
wedgemountainwinery.com

"Walking Through Vines" by Kerry Siderius

"Cluster with Red Leaf" by Kerry Siderius

Apple Pecan Brie

**Contributed by Kristen Wood,
Icicle Ridge Winery, page 12.**

Prep time: 10 minutes
Cook time: 8 minutes
Serves: 8

- 1/2 cup butter (1 stick)
- 1/3 cup brown sugar
- 1/3 cup white sugar
- 1 Granny Smith apple, diced
- 1/3 cup golden raisins
- 1/2 cup pecans, chopped
- 1 tablespoon lemon juice
- 1 wheel Brie cheese

Wine Pairing Suggestions:

Icicle Ridge Winery Ice Riesling

Pasek Cellars Blackberry Dessert Wine

Wine Tip:

Typically a wine should be sweeter than the food it's paired with. Try this recipe with an ice wine or dessert wine.

Combine butter, brown sugar, white sugar, apple, golden raisins, pecans and lemon juice in a saucepan over medium-high heat. Bring to a boil and let boil for a few minutes. Pour the warm sauce over Brie and serve with crackers.

For best results, make the sauce ahead of time and warm it up when ready to serve.

Beecher Hill Roasted Grapes

Contributed by Pamela Kiehn,
Beecher Hill House, page 107.

Prep time: 10 minutes
Cook time: 15 minutes
Serves: 6-8

WINE PAIRING SUGGESTION:
Cascadia Winery Roussanne

- 2 cups seedless grapes, washed, stemmed and dried
- 1/4 cup olive oil
- 1 tablespoon fresh thyme, chopped
- 1/4 teaspoon salt
- 1/4 teaspoon pepper
- Juice from 1 fresh lemon
- Goat cheese or Brie

Preheat oven to 350°F. Toss the grapes with olive oil, thyme, salt and pepper in a medium bowl. Place the grapes in a parchment-covered rimmed baking pan.

Roast for about 15 minutes. Remove and sprinkle with lemon juice. Serve with crackers and your favorite goat cheese, Brie or other soft cheese.

Recipe Tip
Experiment using other herbs in place of thyme, such as flat-leaf parsley or rosemary.

Gorgonzola Balsamic Fruit Plate

Contributed by Taelor Feinberg, The Oil and Vinegar Cellar, page 109.

This is a wonderful appetizer to serve to guests with a glass of wine before dinner. Crisp, tart apples and juicy pears topped with toasted walnuts, Gorgonzola, and aged balsamic vinegar make a perfect combination of flavors and textures.

WINE PAIRING SUGGESTION:
Pasek Cellars Muscat Canelli

Prep time: 10 minutes
Cook time: 5-7 minutes
Serves: 4

- 1/4 cup walnut halves, very roughly chopped
- 1 Granny Smith or Pink Lady apple, cored and sliced
- 1 Bosc or d'Anjou pear, cored and sliced
- 1/4 cup Gorgonzola cheese, crumbled
- 2 tablespoons high quality aged balsamic vinegar
    (Vanilla 18-year Aged Balsamic Vinegar recommended)

Toast the walnuts in a dry sauté pan over medium-high heat, stirring until evenly browned and fragrant, about 5-7 minutes. Set aside.

Place the apples and pears around a serving plate, layering and interchanging the slices as you go. Sprinkle the crumbled Gorgonzola and walnuts over the apples and pears. Drizzle the balsamic vinegar over the top. Serve and enjoy!

<u>*Recipe Tips*</u>
Use goat cheese, St. André, or perhaps a wedge of Brie to spread on the sliced fruit. You can buy all these cheeses locally at the Cheesemonger's Shop in Leavenworth, page 107.

Mushroom, Tomme & Roasted Tomato Crostini

Contributed by Chef de Cuisine Kathy Schmidt, Mountain Home Lodge, page 109.

A delicious appetizer featuring the bounty of the local farmers, sheep dairy and perhaps the forest! The ingredients can be prepped ahead of time and put together when you are ready to serve the crostini.

> **WINE PAIRING SUGGESTIONS:**
> *Boudreaux Cellars Frangio*
> *La Toscana Winery Ellie Kay's Sangiovese*
> *Ryan Patrick Vineyards Rock Island Red Blend*

Prep time: 20-30 minutes
Cook time: 50 minutes
Serves: 6-8

- 6 tablespoons extra virgin olive oil
- 4 large garlic cloves, minced, divided
- 1 tablespoon fresh rosemary, finely chopped
- 1 teaspoon kosher salt
- 1 teaspoon black pepper
- 1-1/2 lbs. organic plum tomatoes (about 6), quartered lengthwise
- 1 fresh baguette, sliced into 12-16 1/2 inch thick diagonal slices
- 1 tablespoon olive oil
- 1 cup chopped fresh mushrooms: chanterelle, crimini, oyster, lobster, etc.
- 4 teaspoons shallots, chopped fine
- 1/8 teaspoon kosher salt
- 1/8 teaspoon black pepper
- 2 teaspoons butter
- 6 oz. tomme, shaved or shredded
  (Alpine Lakes sheep tomme recommended)
- Salt and pepper to taste
- 1/2 cup basil leaves, stems removed, cut into thin ribbons
  (chiffonade style)

Preheat oven to 425°F. In a large bowl, whisk together olive oil, garlic, rosemary, kosher salt and pepper. Add the tomato quarters and gently stir to coat. Let stand 5 minutes while you line a rimmed baking sheet with aluminum foil.

Lift tomatoes from the marinade and arrange, cut side down, on the baking sheet. Set aside the tomato marinade for later use.

recipe continues on page 28

Mushroom, Tomme & Roasted Tomato Crostini (continued)

continued from page 27

Roast the tomatoes in the oven until the skin is blistered and they are very tender, about 30-35 minutes. Cool tomatoes on the baking sheet at room temperature. Keep the oven on to bake the baguette for the crostini.

Arrange the sliced baguette on another rimmed baking sheet. Brush the top of each with the extra tomato marinade, saving 2 tablespoons of the marinade for later use. Bake until golden, 10-12 minutes. Set aside to cool on the sheet.

In an medium skillet, heat 1 tablespoon olive oil over medium-high heat. Sauté the mushrooms and shallots 4-6 minutes until soft. Season lightly with salt and pepper. Remove from pan and set aside to cool.

Heat a medium skillet over medium-high heat. Add the prepared mushroom mixture and remaining garlic and sauté for 2-3 minutes until the garlic becomes fragrant but not browned. Add the last two tablespoons of tomato marinade and cook for a few more minutes to reduce the liquid. Lower the heat to medium and add the butter and half of the tomme, heating just to melt the cheese. Remove from heat.

Sprinkle the remaining tomme evenly on top of the baked crostini baguette. Spoon the hot mushroom mixture onto the crostini. Top with the room-temperature roasted tomatoes and garnish with basil chiffonade.

Recipe Tips
- *Basil darkens once handled, so cut the basil into ribbons at service time to retain the pretty color.*
- *Tomme is a cheese type and the generic name of a type of cheese made mostly in the French Alps and in Switzerland. Tommes are usually created from the left over skim milk, generally making them lower in fat than regular cheeses.*
- *Several Wenatchee and Leavenworth Farmer's Market vendors offer wonderful seasonal organic vegetables, such as Tierra Farm or Gibbs Farm.*

Perfectly Pesto Cheesecake

**Contributed by Julie Moyles,
La Toscana Winery, page 13.**

This savory hors-d'oeuvre is a great spread on crackers. It was originally published in Simply Classic, *a Northwest cookbook by the Junior League of Seattle, page 108.*

Prep time: 30 minutes
Cook time: 45-55 minutes
Cooling time: 1-2 hours
Serves: 12-18

> **_Wine Pairing Suggestions:_**
> *La Toscana Annika's Riesling*
> *Silvara Vineyards Pinot Grigio*

Crust
- 1/4 cup fine, dry breadcrumbs
- 1 tablespoon butter, softened
- 2 tablespoons Parmesan cheese, grated

Filling
- 2 8 oz. packages cream cheese, softened
- 1 cup ricotta cheese
- 1/2 cup grated Parmesan cheese
- 1/2 teaspoon salt
- 1/8 teaspoon cayenne pepper
- 3 large eggs
- 1/2 cup pesto
- 1/3 cup pine nuts

Preheat oven to 325°F. Grease the bottom and sides of an 8-9 inch spring form pan.

Mix the breadcrumbs with butter and Parmesan cheese. Coat the inside of the springform pan with the crust, patting evenly into place.

Using an electric mixer, mix cream cheese, ricotta, Parmesan, salt and cayenne pepper until well blended. Add eggs, one at a time, beating well after each addition.

Transfer half the filling mixture to a medium bowl. Mix the pesto into the remaining half and pour over the crust, smoothing the top. Carefully pour the plain filling over pesto mixture and sprinkle with pine nuts.

Bake on the center rack until the outer edges start to brown and the middle firms up – about 45-50 minutes. Cool completely. Run a small, sharp knife around edges to loosen, then release springform sides. Garnish with fresh basil sprigs and surround with crackers.

Recipe Tip
- *For a firmer end result, add more ricotta cheese.*
- *For crispier pine nuts, sprinkle them on the cheesecake 10 minutes before it has finished baking.*

SALSA VERDE

Contributed by Cappy Bond & Price Gledhill, South Restaurant, page 110.

Prep time: 10 minutes
Cook time: 10 minutes
Chill time: 1 hour
Serves: 10

- 12 tomatillos, peeled and cut in half
- 1 whole onion, cut in half
- 4 cloves garlic
- 1/2 head romaine lettuce, roughly chopped
- 3 serrano peppers, seeds removed
- 1/2 cup cilantro (1 bunch)
- 1/8 teaspoon salt

WINE PAIRING SUGGESTIONS:
Cascadia Winery Roussanne

Stemilt Creek Winery Sweet Adelaide White Blend

Heat a fry pan or griddle on the stove to medium heat. You do not need oil. Place the tomatillos and onion, cut side down, in the pan and let cook until they turn brown and the tomatillos begin to soften.

Once the tomatillos and onion are browned, put them in a blender or food processor with the garlic, lettuce, peppers, cilantro and salt. Blend until smooth, but be careful – the salsa will be HOT!

For best results, chill and serve with chips, over enchiladas or with quesadillas.

Recipe Tip
Tomatillos are a tart green tomato with a papery covering that are used in many Mexican salsas. They are available at most grocery stores in the produce section in late summer and early autumn.

Sweet & Savory Pineapple Salsa

**Contributed by Marlies Egberding,
The Savory Table, page 110.**

Prep time: 30 minutes
Cook time: 15 minutes
Chill time: 1-2 hours
Serves: 6

> **WINE PAIRING SUGGESTIONS:**
> *Pasek Cellars Pineapple Wine*

- 2 cups pineapple wine (Pasek Cellars Pineapple Wine recommended) OR pineapple juice
- 1 tablespoon sugar (omit if using pineapple juice)
- 1/2 cup blueberries
- 1/2 cup sweet onion, chopped
- 4 cups pineapple, chopped (1/2 fresh pineapple)
- 1/4 medium red pepper, chopped
- 1/2 medium orange pepper, chopped
- 2 tomatoes, seeded and chopped
- 1/3 cup cilantro
- 1/4 teaspoon black pepper
- 1/2 teaspoon cumin
- Pinch cayenne pepper

Heat the pineapple wine or pineapple juice over medium heat, adding the sugar if using wine. Slowly reduce, stirring occasionally, until there is about 1/2 cup of sauce - about 15 minutes.

Meanwhile, combine blueberries, onion, pineapple, red pepper, orange pepper, tomatoes and cilantro in a bowl. Mix in the pepper, cumin and cayenne.

Once the reduction is done, mix into the salsa and refrigerate for 1-2 hours before serving as an appetizer with chips or over grilled pork tenderloin.

Walnut Crusted Brie with Apple Cherry Chutney

Contributed by Stemilt Creek Winery, page 17.

Prep time: 40 minutes
Cook time: 30 minutes
Serves: 6-8

- 5 oz. wedge Brie (skin on)
- 3 tablespoons unsalted butter
- 1-1/2 tablespoons shallots, minced
- 1/3 cup brown sugar, firmly packed
- 1 teaspoon fresh orange zest
- 1 Fuji apple, cored and finely diced
- 1 cup fresh Stemilt sweet cherries, halved and pitted
- 2 tablespoons dried apricots, minced
- 3 tablespoons golden raisins
- 1/8 teaspoon ground allspice
- 1 teaspoon apple cider vinegar
- 1/8 teaspoon white pepper
- 2 tablespoons fresh lemon juice (Meyer lemon recommended)
- 1 cup walnuts, very finely chopped or ground
- 1 egg
- 1/8 teaspoon salt
- 1 teaspoon 2 percent milk (or heavy cream, as preferred)
- Baguette bread, sliced and toasted

> **_Wine Pairing Suggestions:_**
> *Cascadia Winery Apple Wine*
> *Stemilt Creek Winery Sweet Adelaide White Blend*

Preheat oven to 350°F. Place Brie wedge in freezer for 15 minutes.

Meanwhile, melt butter in a large saucepan over medium-high heat. Add shallots; cook until softened, about 2 minutes. Add brown sugar and orange zest. Cook until sugar is completely dissolved. Add apples, cherries, apricots, raisins, allspice, apple cider vinegar, and white pepper.

Bring mixture to a low boil and simmer, stirring occasionally, until liquid has reduced by about half and sauce has thickened, about 15 minutes. Remove from heat, stir in lemon juice, cover and set aside.

Place chopped nuts in a shallow dish. Crack egg into a separate shallow dish. Add salt and milk to the egg and whisk until well combined. Remove Brie from freezer and dip in egg wash, coating cheese on all surfaces. Transfer to walnut mix and turn to coat with nuts, gently pressing to ensure coverage. Bake on a pan with sides for 15 minutes.

Toast baguette slices and arrange on tray with baked Brie. Spoon apple cherry chutney into a bowl and serve immediately with cheese and toast.

Notes

"Pinot Gris" by Kerry Siderius

"Peshastin Pinnacles" by Kerry Siderius

BLEU CHEESE PEAR SALAD

**Contributed by Kristen Wood,
Icicle Ridge Winery, page 12.**

*"We love to use any of our pears in this salad, but our favorite has to be the Bosc pear. The color and texture of the Bosc is absolutely perfect!"
– Kristen Wood*

**Prep time: 10 minutes
Cook time: 5 minutes
Serves: 4**

Dressing:
- 1/4 cup olive oil
- 5 large basil leaves, roughly chopped
- 3 cloves garlic, minced
- 1/4 teaspoon salt
- 1 tablespoon honey

Salad
- 8 large romaine leaves, torn
- 3/4 cup Bleu cheese, crumbled
- 2 pears, peeled cored and diced (Bosc pears recommended)
- 3/4 cup walnuts or pecans, chopped and toasted

WINE PAIRING SUGGESTIONS:
Icicle Ridge Winery The Blondes Gewürztraminer

PAIRING TIP:
Bleu cheese can overwhelm white wine. Keep this in mind if another wine pairing doesn't seem to work.

Combine olive oil, basil, garlic, salt and honey in a jar and shake until honey is mixed in. Let sit for 5-10 minutes to release the basil flavor from the leaves.

Toast the walnuts or pecans in a dry pan over medium high heat until browned.

Mix romaine leaves, Bleu cheese and pears in a bowl with nuts.

Strain the basil leaves out of the dressing.

Pour dressing over the salad and toss well before serving.

Beet Salad

Contributed by Executive Chef Daniel Carr and Chef de Cuisine Steve Coin, Visconti's Ristorante, page 110.

Prep time: 15 minutes
Cook time: 45-60 minutes
Serves: 2

- 2 large red and/or golden beets
- 3 tablespoons olive oil, divided
- 1 tablespoon red wine vinegar
- 1 teaspoon honey
- 3 cups arugula
- 4 tablespoons aged balsamic vinegar
- 1/2 cup goat cheese, Gorgonzola OR Roquefort
- 1/4 cup toasted walnuts

WINE PAIRING SUGGESTIONS:
Ryan Patrick Vineyards Reserve Chardonnay
Ryan Patrick Vineyards Rosé
Swakane Winery Estate Rosé of Cabernet Franc

Preheat oven to 450°F. Cut the greens off the beets, drizzle them in 1 tablespoon olive oil, wrap them in aluminum foil and bake for 45-50 minutes, or until easily pierced with a fork. Allow to cool slightly; remove the skins and dice.

To create the dressing, mix red wine vinegar, 2 tablespoons olive oil and honey.

Place the arugula in a large bowl and add the diced beets. Drizzle with the dressing, top with the aged balsamic and garnish with the goat cheese and toasted walnuts.

Chorizo Yam Bisque

**Contributed by Dave Hambleton,
The Cheesemonger's Shop, page 107.**

This is a great fall or winter soup – the smoky chorizo really sets off the rich, creamy yams. For a cooler summertime alternative, chill it and garnish with cilantro and limes. You can also use sweet potatoes, but the orange yams are more colorful! – Dave Hambleton

Prep time: 20 minutes
Cook time: 1 hour
Serves: 4

Wine Pairing Suggestions:
Boudreaux Cellars Syrah
Eagle Creek Adler Weiss
Eagle Creek Winery Syrah

- 2 lbs. yams, peeled and cubed (about 4)
- 2 tablespoons olive oil, divided
- 1 onion, diced
- 2 stalks celery, diced
- 1 garlic clove, minced
- 2 tablespoons ginger root, grated
- 12-16 oz. package Mexican chorizo (pork)
- 1/2 teaspoon cinnamon
- Salt and pepper to taste
- 4 cups chicken stock
- 1/2 cup whipping cream
- 3 tablespoons maple syrup (grade B recommended)

Preheat oven to 400°F. Cube yams into 1 inch pieces and toss with 1 tablespoon olive oil. Roast in the oven for 40 minutes.

Meanwhile, heat the remaining tablespoon of oil in a soup pot. Sauté onions, celery, garlic and ginger over medium heat until soft. Set aside until yams are done.

Cut the casing off of the chorizo and sauté in a separate frying pan until cooked through; drain off fat.

When the yams are tender enough to stab through with a fork, add them to the onions and celery in the soup pot. Add cinnamon, salt and pepper. Add the chicken stock and simmer for 15 minutes.

Pour yam mixture into blender and puree until smooth, but be careful – it will be HOT! Return to pot and add cooked chorizo. Ladle into individual bowls.

Stir cream and maple syrup together and drizzle over the top of each bowl. If you are feeling really fancy, whip the cream and fold in the syrup before dolloping onto the bisque.

GAZPACHO BLANCO

Contributed by Joanne Saliby, author of the Wenatchee World *Living Well* blog, page 109.

"When we lived in Georgia we met a couple who became good friends. He was from Turkey. One evening they had us over for a Turkish dinner. One dish was a cold cucumber and yogurt soup. Cucumbers and yogurt? Oh dear. But we were polite and ate some. It was good! It has been a summer standard ever since. Served in chilled, clear glass bowls, it's very refreshing on a warm day as a light lunch, or as a first course for dinner."
- Joanne Saliby

WINE PAIRING SUGGESTIONS:
Eagle Creek White Riesling
Wedge Mountain Winery Dry Riesling

Prep time: 10 minutes
Chill time: 2 hours
Serves: 4

- 2 lbs. cucumbers, peeled and chopped (about 4)
- 1 garlic clove, pressed
- 2 cups low sodium chicken broth, divided
- 3 cups plain yogurt (low fat or regular)
- 3 tablespoons apple cider vinegar
- Salt and pepper to taste

Garnish
- Diced tomato
- Sliced green onions
- Parsley
- Chives

Process cucumber, garlic and 1 cup chicken broth in a blender until smooth. A blender works better than a food processor for this.

Pour into bowl, stir in remaining chicken broth, yogurt, vinegar, salt and pepper.

Cover and chill at least two hours. Serve in chilled bowls and sprinkle with desired garnish.

Grilled Ahi Tuna Salad

**Contributed by Julie Moyles,
La Toscana, page 13.**

Prep time: 15 minutes
Cook time: 4-8 minutes
Serves: 2

Wine Pairing Suggestions:
'37 Cellars Columbia Valley Chardonnay

Crayelle Cellars Dry Riesling

Soy-Lime Vinaigrette
- 1/4 cup rice vinegar
- 1/4 cup low sodium soy sauce
- 1/4 cup fresh lime juice
- 2 teaspoons dark sesame oil
- 1 teaspoon lemon zest
- 1 teaspoon fresh ginger, grated
- 2 cloves garlic, minced

Salad
- 1 fresh raw tuna steak
- 2 cups arugula or mixed spring greens
- 1/4 cup edamame (soybeans)
- 1/4 cup water chestnuts, chopped or sliced
- 1/4 cup papaya or mango
- 1 tablespoon toasted sesame seeds

Thoroughly blend all the ingredients of the vinaigrette well. Set aside.

Grill the tuna 2-4 minutes on each side before cutting into thin slices. Alternatively, you can pan-fry the tuna in sesame oil over medium-high heat for 2-4 minutes a side.

Arrange greens on a plate and sprinkle with soybeans and water chestnuts. Top with grilled tuna slices, and mango or papaya.

Garnish with toasted sesame seeds and drizzle with vinaigrette.

Gumbo

Contributed by Rob Newsom, Boudreaux Cellars, page 7.

Prep time: 1 hour 15 minutes
Stock cook time: 1-3 hours
Cook time: 1-3 hours
Serves: 10

WINE PAIRING SUGGESTIONS:
Boudreaux Cellars Chardonnay
Crayelle Cellars Dry Riesling
Silvara Vineyards Pinot Grigio

- 4 lbs. peeled shrimp, shells reserved
- 1 gallon + 4 cups water (20 cups)
- 1 cup canola or safflower oil
- 1 cup rice flour
- 2 large onions, sliced
- 10 cloves garlic, sliced
- 1/2 green bell pepper, chopped
- 3 stalks celery, chopped
- 1 lb. okra, chopped (3-4 cups)
- 1/2 cup butter (1 stick)
- 2 teaspoons Worcestershire sauce
- 1 tablespoon salt
- 2 teaspoons black pepper
- 2 teaspoons cayenne pepper
- 4 bay leaves
- 1 teaspoon dried thyme
- 1 teaspoon dried basil
- 1 teaspoon sweet paprika
- 12 oz. can whole tomatoes, OR 8 fresh tomatoes, halved
- 1 lb. crab meat OR 1 lb. peeled crawfish tails
- 2 lb. package rice

Peel the shrimp, rinse and refrigerate. In a 2-gallon pot, add shrimp shells to 20 cups boiling water. Boil uncovered on medium-high heat for 1-3 hours. After cooking, strain out the shells and discard them.

Heat the oil in a large skillet over medium heat. When the oil is hot enough that a droplet of water sizzles in it, quickly stir in the flour. Cook the roux, stirring constantly, until flour is quite brown – about 10 minutes. Add the onions, garlic, bell pepper, celery, okra, and butter and cook until the vegetables have sautéed slightly, about 5 minutes.

Pour 12 cups of shrimp stock into a large and heavy pot (not cast iron). Add the roux/veggie mix. Add Worcestershire sauce, salt, pepper, cayenne, bay leaves, thyme, basil, paprika and tomatoes. Cover and simmer on medium-low heat for 1-3 hours; the longer the better. Add the shrimp and crab 5-7 minutes before serving. The shrimp is ready when it turns pink. Remove bay leaves and adjust seasonings as needed.

Cook rice according to package directions, using the remaining shrimp stock and additional water as needed. Serve gumbo over rice with French bread.

Tarragon & Crab Stuffed Tomatoes

Contributed by Julie Moyles, La Toscana Winery, page 13.

The tomatoes, with a slice of frittata and lightly grilled rustic bread, make an easy summer brunch meal. For best results, make the filling the night before to allow the flavors to marry.

Prep time: 30 minutes
Serves: 4

> **WINE PAIRING SUGGESTIONS:**
> *Ryan Patrick Vineyards Naked Chardonnay*
>
> *Wedge Mountain Winery Pinot Grigio*

- 4 medium tomatoes
- 1/2 lb. fresh crab meat
- 1/3 cup fresh fennel bulb, chopped
- 1/4 cup yellow bell pepper, chopped
- 2 green onions, trimmed and thinly sliced
- 1/4 cup reduced fat mayonnaise
- 1 tablespoon fresh tarragon, chopped
- 1 tablespoon fresh lemon juice
- 1/4 teaspoon salt
- 1/4 teaspoon fresh ground black pepper

Garnish
- Parsley sprig OR fresh basil leaf

Cut a 1/2 inch slice off the stem end of each tomato. With a small spoon, gently scoop out and discard pulp to create a hollow shell.

Turn tomatoes upside down on a plate lined with paper towels and allow to drain for at least 25 minutes.

Combine crab meat, fennel, bell pepper, green onions, mayonnaise, tarragon, lemon juice, salt and pepper in a medium bowl. Stir to combine.

Spoon crab mixture into tomato shells.

Garnish with a parsley sprig or a fresh basil leaf.

"Autumn Leaves" by Kerry Siderius

"Autumn Leaves" by Kerry Siderius

APPLE SWEET POTATO ROAST PORK

**Contributed by Kristen Wood,
Icicle Ridge Winery, page 12.**

This pork roast is baked with all the right fall and cold weather ingredients: honey, orange juice, apple juice concentrate, brown sugar, sweet potatoes, and apples. It is a great "white" meat to serve over the holidays.

**Prep time: 30 minutes
Cook time: 1 hour 30 minutes
Serves: 8-10**

> **WINE PAIRING SUGGESTIONS:**
> *Eagle Creek White Riesling*
> *Wedge Mountain Winery Dry Lemberger*

- 2 tablespoons vegetable oil
- 3 to 4 lb. boneless pork loin roast, fat trimmed
- 1/3 cup honey
- 1/4 cup orange juice
- 1/4 cup frozen apple juice concentrate, thawed
- 2 teaspoons ground black pepper (or 1 teaspoon for less "zip")
- 1 tablespoon brown sugar, packed
- 3 large sweet potatoes, peeled and quartered
- 3 large apples, cored and quartered

Preheat the oven to 350°F. Coat a large ovenproof Dutch oven with vegetable oil and place on the stove on high heat.

When a droplet of water sizzles in the oil, add the pork roast. Cook, turning, until all sides are browned, about 6 minutes. Remove from heat.

In a medium bowl, combine the honey, orange juice, apple juice concentrate, pepper and brown sugar. Spoon over the pork roast in the Dutch oven. Place the sweet potatoes around the pork.

Cover and bake until the pork registers 150°F on a thermometer, or 20 minutes per pound: about an hour and 20 minutes for a 4 pound roast.

About 20 minutes before it's done, place the apple quarters around the pork. Bake, uncovered, basting frequently, until the apples are just tender.

Let the pork stand for 10 minutes before slicing. Serve pork roast in slices with the sweet potatoes and apples.

ARTIST'S VACATION GREEK LAMB

Contributed by Kerry Siderius, watercolor artist, page 108.

"When I finally go to Greece, this is what I imagine the food will taste like! This recipe always gets rave reviews, especially in August and September when I have fresh basil." - Kerry Siderius

Prep time: 45 minutes
Marinate time: 7 hours to overnight
Cook time: 25 minutes
Serves: 4

WINE PAIRING SUGGESTIONS:
'37 Cellars Cabernet Sauvignon
Boudreaux Cellars Cabernet Sauvignon
Silvara Vineyards Malbec

- 1 cup Dijon mustard
- 1-1/2 cups fresh lemon juice
- 4 2 oz. cans anchovies, drained, oil reserved, anchovies chopped
- 3/4 cup extra virgin olive oil
- 2 cups (packed) fresh basil, chopped
- 1 cup shallots OR red and yellow onions, chopped
- 1 leg of lamb, ALL fat trimmed, deboned & butterflied
- Salt and pepper
- 1 lb. small red potatoes, peeled
- 1 lb. mushrooms, halved or whole if small
- 1 lb. fresh string beans, cut into 1 inch pieces

Garnish
- Fresh baby spinach leaves (about three handfuls)
- Fresh basil sprigs

In a food processor or blender, mix mustard, lemon juice, anchovy oil, anchovies, olive oil, basil and shallots or onions. Blend until smooth. Separate out 2 cups of the marinade for the potato salad dressing and refrigerate.

Season the lamb with salt and pepper. Place the lamb in a large baking dish and pour the rest of the marinade over the lamb, coating all sides. Cover and refrigerate overnight, or for at least 7 hours.

When ready to cook, set out the 2 cups of dressing to bring to room temperature. Place lamb on the grill and cook over medium heat until the temperature reaches 135°F at the thickest part, about 12 minutes per side. Brush with the extra marinade while cooking. Transfer to a platter and let stand for 15 minutes.

Bring a pot of salted water to boil and add the potatoes. Cook about 10 minutes, then add the green beans. When the potatoes and green beans are almost done – about 5 to 7 minutes – add mushrooms. Drain and toss with enough room-temperature dressing to coat, saving the rest to use as dip for the lamb.

Line a large platter with baby spinach leaves. Place the rested lamb on top of spinach leaves, garnish with basil sprigs and surround with warm potato salad.

Recipe Tip
Don't be afraid of the anchovies – they add depth of flavor but not a fishy taste.

Balsamic Glazed Salmon

**Contributed by Taelor Feinberg,
The Oil and Vinegar Cellar, page 109.**

This recipe offers a wonderful balance between savory, sweet, and tart flavors. Best yet, it's easy, healthy, and delicious!

**Prep time: 20 minutes
Cook time: 8-12 minutes
Serves: 2**

<u>**Wine Pairing Suggestion:**</u>
Ryan Patrick Vineyards Rosé

- 2 salmon fillets (about 4 oz. each)
- 1/4 teaspoon salt
- 1/2 teaspoon fresh ground black pepper
- 1 teaspoon dried rosemary
- 2 tablespoons good quality aged balsamic vinegar
    (Cinnamon Peach 18-year Aged Balsamic Vinegar recommended)
- 2 teaspoons brown sugar

Preheat oven to 350°F. Pat the salmon fillets dry with a paper towel. Rub the salt, pepper, and rosemary over the salmon. Let sit for 10 minutes. Place the fillets on a baking sheet and bake for 6-8 minutes.

Combine the balsamic vinegar and brown sugar in a small bowl, stirring to mix.

Remove salmon from the oven and change the oven setting to broil. Brush the balsamic brown sugar mixture on the top of the salmon. Broil for 3 minutes, allowing the mixture to crisp. The salmon is done when it can be easily flaked with a fork.

Serve with fresh salad greens or sautéed asparagus.

<u>*Recipe Tip*</u>
Try adding a pinch of ground cinnamon to the rub to give it an extra boost of spice.

Butternut Squash Ravioli with Sage Butter

Contributed by Executive Chef Daniel Carr and Chef de Cuisine Steve Coin, Visconti's Ristorante, page 110.

Prep time: 1 hour 15 minutes
Cook time: 50 minutes
Serves: 6

Filling
- 3 to 4 lbs. butternut squash OR delicata pumpkin (about 3 cups cooked)
- 1 tablespoon extra virgin olive oil
- 1 teaspoon kosher salt
- 1 teaspoon ground black pepper
- 1-2/3 cups Italian breadcrumbs
- 1-2/3 cups grated Parmesan cheese
- 3 large eggs
- 1-1/2 teaspoons ground nutmeg
- 1-1/2 teaspoons ground white pepper
- 1-1/2 teaspoons ground black pepper

Pasta dough
- Pasta machine (optional)
- Ravioli tray (optional)
- 1/2 tablespoon kosher salt for boiling water
- 3-3/4 cups all-purpose flour
- 5 large eggs
- 1/2 tablespoon kosher salt
- 1 tablespoon extra virgin olive oil

Sage butter
- 1 cup unsalted butter (2 sticks)
- 18 fresh sage leaves

Garnish
- 1/2 cup Parmesan

> **WINE PAIRING SUGGESTIONS:**
> Eagle Creek Winery Chardonnay
> Ryan Patrick Vineyards Reserve Chardonnay
> Silvara Vineyards Chardonnay

Preheat the oven to 400°F. Cut the squash or pumpkin in half lengthwise and remove the seeds. Place the halves face-up on a cookie sheet, drizzle with olive oil and add salt and pepper. Bake the squash for 30-45 minutes, or until a fork easily goes through the flesh.

continued on page 52

Butternut Squash Ravioli (continued)

continued from page 50

Meanwhile, start the pasta dough by placing the flour in a mound in the middle of a pastry board or work surface. Dig a well in the center of the mound and break the eggs into it. Beat the eggs with a fork, gradually incorporating the flour into the eggs. You may not need all of the flour – it depends on how much the eggs can absorb. As soon as you have a consistent bundle, start kneading the dough using the palms of your hands. Using a pastry or dough scraper, scrape the board and incorporate all the pellets of dough. Continue kneading and folding the dough until you obtain a smooth, elastic ball – at least 15 minutes or 10 minutes if using a hand-cranked pasta machine. After kneading, let the dough rest for at least 30 minutes.

After the squash is done, let it cool for about 10 minutes or until you can comfortably scoop the flesh into a bowl. Add the breadcrumbs, Parmesan, eggs, nutmeg, and white and black pepper.

After the dough has rested, cut it into 4 wedges and roll them one at a time through a pasta machine, or roll them out with a rolling pin until they are thin sheets.

Bring a large pot of water to a boil with 1/2 tablespoon of kosher salt.

If using a ravioli tray, press a sheet of dough over the ravioli tray and gently press the dough into the depressions. Alternatively, cut the pasta into 1-1/2 to 2 inch squares, or cut out circles with a cookie cutter.

Place about a tablespoon of filling in each depression. Dip a finger in a glass of water and run it along the lines where the pasta sheets will stick together. The water creates a tight seal and prevents the pasta from breaking when boiled.

Using the ravioli tray, cover the squares with another sheet of dough, pressing down along the edges to seal. Roll a rolling pin over the tray, gently at first to let any air escape, then more firmly to seal the pasta together and cut the raviolis along their edges.

To form the pasta without a ravioli tray, place a tablespoon of filling in the middle of the square or circle, dip your finger in water and run it along the edge of the pasta. Place another square or circle of pasta over the filling and gently press the edges together, making sure to create a tight seal. Repeat the process until all the dough is used.

To create the sage butter, melt the butter in a saucepan over medium heat, add the sage leaves and let them cook until they begin to crisp: about 30 seconds.

Gently add the raviolis to the boiling water and cook for 3-4 minutes. Place the ravioli in bowls, drizzle with the sage butter and garnish with Parmesan cheese.

Creamy Smoked Salmon & Asparagus

Contributed by Joanne Saliby, author of the Wenatchee World *Living Well* blog, page 109.

Note: Joanne Saliby created this recipe specifically to pair with Ryan Patrick Vineyard's Reserve Chardonnay.

Prep time: 10 minutes
Cook time: 20 minutes
Serves: 4-6

> **WINE PAIRING SUGGESTIONS:**
> '37 Cellars Columbia Valley Chardonnay
> Boudreaux Cellars Chardonnay
> Ryan Patrick Vineyards Reserve Chardonnay

- 1 lb. package multi-grain pasta
- 1 tablespoon grapeseed oil OR butter
- 1/2 cup onion, thinly sliced
- 1 clove garlic, minced
- 1 cup dry white wine
- 2 cups cream (100 percent cream recommended, not ultra-pasturized)
- 1/4 teaspoon salt, or less to taste
- Several grinds white pepper
- 1/8 teaspoon cayenne pepper
- 1/2 teaspoon lemon zest
- 1/2 lb. moist smoked salmon, torn into bite-sized pieces
- 2 cups asparagus, cut into 1 inch pieces

Garnish
- 2 tablespoons fresh chives, minced

Heat water in large pot and cook pasta according to package directions.

Meanwhile, heat oil or butter in a medium sauté pan. Add onion and garlic. Cook on low for several minutes or until softened; do not brown. Remove from heat and allow to rest for a few minutes.

Return to burner, add wine and turn heat to medium-high. Simmer until wine is reduced by about half. Add cream, salt, pepper, cayenne, lemon zest and salmon. Remove from heat to rest while steaming the asparagus. If it thickens too much for your taste, add 1 tablespoon hot water.

Steam or blanch asparagus until barely tender, about 5 minutes. Drain and add to salmon in cream.

To serve, plate the pasta and top with desired amount of sauce and asparagus. Sprinkle with chives.

ENTRÉES

DAVE'S MAC & CHEESE

Contributed by Dave Hambleton,
The Cheesemonger's Shop, page 107.

"As the owner of a cheese shop, I am often asked for a macaroni and cheese recipe. This combines a number of recipes. I have seen wide variations in proportions and they all seem to come out pretty well (although I admit I always seem to jack up the cheese quantities). The important thing here is to learn the technique and have fun trying different cheese combinations! Try a sharp cheddar, or something mild and creamy like Havarti or Butterkase. The possibilities are endless!"
- Dave Hambleton

> **WINE PAIRING SUGGESTIONS:**
> Eagle Creek Winery Cabernet Sauvignon
> Pasek Cellars Chardonnay
>
> **WINE TIP:**
> Soft cheeses generally pair well with white wines, while hard cheeses pair best with reds.

Prep time: 30 minutes
Cook time: 45 minutes
Serves: 3-4

- 1 lb. penne pasta, cooked and drained
- 1 onion, diced
- 1 clove garlic, minced
- 1/2 cup butter (1 stick)
- 4 cups milk
- 1/4 to 1/3 cup flour
- 1/8 teaspoon cayenne pepper
- 1 tablespoon Dijon Mustard
- Fresh nutmeg - just a few grates (optional)
- 4-5 cups cheese, grated (any kind)
- 1 cup seasoned breadcrumbs
- 1/2 cup Pecorino Romano cheese
- Salt and pepper to taste

Cook the pasta according to package directions, leaving it a bit on the underdone side. Drain well.

Preheat the oven to 350° F. While the pasta is cooking, sauté the onions and garlic in butter in a large skillet over medium heat for 5-6 minutes. It seems like too much butter, but it makes a thicker sauce.

Warm the milk in a saucepan.

Sprinkle the flour over the cooked onions and cook the resulting roux for an additional 5-6 minutes, stirring constantly. Stir in warmed milk a little at a time, and heat until just steaming (do not boil). Add cayenne, mustard and nutmeg. Slowly add the cheese, stirring constantly until melted.

Stir in cooked pasta; transfer to greased 9x13 inch glass baking dish. Top with breadcrumbs and grated Pecorino Romano. Bake for 30 minutes. Serve hot.

Feta Mint Lamb Burgers

**Contributed by Kristen Wood,
Icicle Ridge Winery, page 12.**

Prep time: 15 minutes
Cook time: 8-15 minutes
Serves: 4

> **_Wine Pairing Suggestions:_**
> *Icicle Ridge Winery Romanze Blend*
> *Icicle Ridge Winery Merlot*

- 2 cloves garlic
- 1/8 teaspoon salt
- 1/2 teaspoon pepper
- 1/2 cup packed mint leaves, finely chopped
- 1/2 cup crumbled feta cheese
- 1-1/4 lb. ground lamb
- 8 oz. Greek yogurt
- 1 package Ciabatta buns

Prepare a gas grill for direct-heat cooking over medium heat.

Mash garlic to a paste with salt. Gently mix the paste with pepper, mint, and feta.

Divide lamb into 4 equal balls. Make an indentation in center of each one and stuff each with a quarter of the mint mixture. Pinch the well closed and form into a 1 inch thick patty. Season burgers with salt and pepper.

Brush the grill rack with oil. Grill the burgers 8-10 minutes for medium rare or 10-13 minutes for medium, turning once.

Serve on Ciabatta buns with a dollop of Greek yogurt.

Flank Steak Portabella Sandwiches

**Contributed by Kristen Wood,
Icicle Ridge Winery, page 12.**

Prep time: 30 minutes
Marinate time: 1 hour
Cook time: 8-10 minutes
Serves: 6

> ### Wine Pairing Suggestions:
> *Icicle Ridge Winery Syrah*
> *Silvara Vineyards Syrah*
> *Stemilt Creek Winery Estate Syrah*

- 5 cloves minced garlic + 2 cloves sliced, divided
- 1 tablespoon fresh rosemary, chopped
- 1 tablespoon fresh thyme, chopped
- 1-1/2 teaspoons salt
- 2 teaspoons pepper
- 1-1/2 to 2 lbs. flank steak
- 1/4 cup olive oil + 2 tablespoons olive oil, divided
- 1 medium red onion, minced
- 1 cup portabella mushrooms, sliced
- 1/4 cup sweet Marsala wine
- Kosher salt and freshly ground pepper
- 1 tablespoon extra virgin olive oil
- 1 medium Walla Walla sweet onion
- 6 slices (1/2 inch thick) rustic white bread, lightly toasted
- 2 tablespoons Dijon mustard
- 6 oz. Gorgonzola cheese

Combine 3 cloves garlic, rosemary, thyme, salt and pepper. Rub over the steaks. Drizzle 1/4 cup olive oil over meat and let sit at room temperature for 1 hour.

Heat 2 tablespoons of oil over medium-high heat. Add the red onion and remaining 2 cloves minced garlic and sauté 2-3 minutes. Add mushrooms, Marsala wine, salt and pepper. Stir frequently until the mushrooms are cooked through and the liquid has evaporated, about 5-6 minutes. Transfer the mushrooms to a bowl.

Add remaining olive oil to the pan. Sauté Walla Walla sweet onion, salt and pepper over medium-high heat until browned and caramelized, about 5-7 minutes. Add sliced garlic and cook until brown, about 1 minute. Stir into bowl of mushrooms.

Grill steak on high for 4-5 minutes per side. Remove from heat and let rest for 5 minutes. Cut the steak across the grain into thin slices.

Spread toasted bread with mustard and Gorgonzola. Add steak strips to the toast and drizzle with leftover juices. Serve open-faced, topped with mushroom-onion mixture and top with additional Gorgonzola.

Gnocchi with Roasted Tomato Red Pepper Sauce

Contributed by Executive Chef Daniel Carr and Chef de Cuisine Steve Coin, Visconti's Ristorante, page 110.

Prep time: 1 hour
Cook time: 25 minutes
Serves: 4

Roasted Tomato Red Pepper Sauce
- 12 Roma tomatoes, halved
- 1/2 yellow onion, thickly sliced
- 4 cloves garlic, thinly sliced
- 1/4 cup extra virgin olive oil
- 1/4 teaspoon salt
- 1/4 teaspoon ground black pepper
- 1 red bell pepper, cut in half and deseeded
- 1 sprig fresh oregano, chopped
- 2 tablespoons fresh lemon juice
- Salt and pepper to taste

Gnocchi
- Potato ricer or food mill
- 1-1/3 lbs. russet potatoes, peeled (about 1 lb. or 2 cups after ricing)
- 1 tablespoon kosher salt for boiling water
- 3/4 cup flour
- 3/4 teaspoon kosher salt
- 1/4 teaspoon ground nutmeg
- 1 egg

Garnish
- 3/4 cup part skim mozzarella cheese, grated
- 1 cup ricotta cheese
- 2 tablespoons Parmesan cheese, grated
- 2 fresh tomatoes, thinly sliced

Wine Pairing Suggestions:
La Toscana Winery
Ellie Kay's Sangiovese

Wedge Mountain Winery Trois Chevaux Rouges Red Blend

Roasted Tomato Red Pepper Sauce
Preheat the oven to 450°F. Place the tomato halves, onion and garlic in a single layer on a rimmed baking sheet so the juice and oil won't run off. Drizzle with olive oil and salt and pepper. Place the cut and deseeded red pepper on a separate cookie sheet, skin side up. Roast the vegetables until the tomatoes and onion have caramelized and the pepper has blackened – about 15-20 minutes.

continued on page 59

Gnocchi with Roasted Tomato Red Pepper Sauce (continued)

continued from page 57

Remove the pepper from the oven and place it immediately in a plastic bag for 15 minutes to cause the pepper to sweat.

After the pepper has cooled, remove the skin. Put all the vegetables into a food processor or blender with the oregano and lemon juice. Pulse until slightly chunky. Add salt and pepper to taste.

Gnocchi
Bring a pot of water to boil. Cut potatoes into quarters and boil them until soft. Pass through a ricer or food mill and spread out to allow the potatoes to cool and dry out; do not compact them.

Bring another pot of water to boil over high heat. Add kosher salt. Once it's boiling, reduce the temperature to medium high; it should just barely be boiling.

When the processed potatoes are cool enough to touch, place them in a mound and cover with flour. Sprinkle with salt and nutmeg.

Gently create a well in the center of the mound. Crack the egg into the well and mix it completely with a fork. Slowly begin to incorporate the flour and potato mixture until the egg is mixed into the dry ingredients.

Knead LIGHTLY (do not compact) until the dough is dry to the touch – you may need to add additional flour. Roll the dough into a log about 1/2- to 3/4 inch in diameter, then cut the roll into 3/4 inch pieces. Press each piece gently with a fork to flatten.

Drop the gnocchi in the boiling water. They are done when they float to the surface, about 3-4 minutes. Scoop them out with a slotted spoon.

To serve, place the gnocchi in a bowl, cover with sauce and garnish with the cheeses and tomato slices.

Recipe Tip:
To save gnocchi for later use, set up a pan with 2 cups water, 2 cups ice. After you have boiled the gnocchi, place them in the ice bath immediately and let them cool for about 5 minutes. Remove from the ice bath, toss with olive oil, and place on cookie sheets to freeze. Once frozen, they can be put in plastic bags for storage. To reheat, drop the frozen gnocchi into boiling salted water and cook until they float to the surface, about 7-9 minutes.

GRILLED LAMB BURGERS IN RED WINE

Contributed by Joanne Saliby, author of the Wenatchee World *Living Well* blog, page 109.

"In these carb-conscious days, the hamburger, that good old standby for summer grilling, is often served without the bun. While not a follower of low to no carb diets, I have found some pretty good toppings that turn the burger, chop or steak into something more than just meat to be hidden in a bun." – Joanne Saliby

WINE PAIRING SUGGESTIONS:
Bella Terrazza Vineyards Estate Lemberger
Horan Estates Cabernet Sauvignon
Silvara Vineyards 60/40 Red Blend

Prep time: 10 minutes
Cook time: 15 minutes
Serves: 4

- 2 slices bacon
- 1 tablespoon grapeseed or olive oil
- 1/2 large red onion, cut into 1/4 inch pieces
- 1/4 teaspoon kosher salt
- 2 cloves garlic, finely minced
- 1 cup dry red wine
- 1 teaspoon brown sugar
- 1/8 teaspoon red pepper flakes (or to taste)
- 1/4 teaspoon dried or 1/2 teaspoon fresh thyme
- 1-1/4 lb. ground lamb
- 1 tablespoon cold, unsalted butter, cut into 9 cubes

Cook 2 slices of bacon until crisp in a small sauté pan.

Add grapeseed or olive oil to the pan. Add onion and salt and cook slowly on medium-low heat until the onion is softened and beginning to caramelize; do not brown. Add garlic and cook until softened and fragrant. Add wine, brown sugar, red pepper flakes and thyme and increase to medium-high heat. Reduce to about 1/2 cup liquid.

Meanwhile, shape the lamb into four equal patties. Brush the grill rack with oil. Grill the burgers 8-10 minutes for medium rare or 10-13 minutes for medium, turning once.

Whisk butter into sauce, one cube at a time. Crumble the bacon slices into the sauce and serve on your grilled meat.

Hambleton Hominy Casserole

Contributed by Dave Hambleton, The Cheesemonger's Shop, page 107.

"This recipe is like a macaroni and cheese dish—it's ok to substitute freely. It is also fine to try a completely different style of cheese: Jalapeño Havarti, Cave-Aged Gruyere, or even Applewood-Smoked Cheddar. This basic recipe also works well in a crock pot – we feed this to The Cheesemonger's Shop staff on festival weekends!" – Dave Hambleton

WINE PAIRING SUGGESTIONS:
Wedge Mountain Winery Semi Sweet Lemberger

Wedge Mountain Winery Trois Chevaux Rouges Red Blend

WINE TIP:
The more heat in a dish, the sweeter the wine should be.

Prep Time: 20 minutes
Cook time: 15 minutes
Serves: 4

- 4 slices thick bacon
- 1/2 large onion, finely diced
- 2 14.5 oz. cans white hominy, drained
- 2 4 oz. cans diced green chilies, drained
- 6-8 slices pickled jalapeño, diced (more or less to taste)
- 1-1/2 cups sharp cheddar, grated

Garnish
- Cheddar
- Bacon
- Chilies

Preheat oven to 350°F. In a large frying pan, cook the bacon on medium-high until it is lightly brown but not yet crisp, about 5-7 minutes. Remove from skillet and drain all but a couple of tablespoons bacon grease. Once the bacon is cooled, cut into small pieces and set aside.

Sauté the onion in the remaining bacon grease for about 5 minutes, or until soft. Add the hominy and stir for about 2 minutes until warm. Add bacon pieces, chilies, jalapeños, and cheese and stir.

When the cheese is melted, pour the mixture into a greased 10x6 inch casserole dish. If desired, garnish with additional cheese, bacon, and green chilies.

Bake for 15 minutes, or until hot and heated through.

Herb's Sweet & Tangy Salmon Sauce

Contributed by Pamela Kiehn, Beecher Hill House, page 107.

Prep time: 5 minutes
Cook time: 10 minutes
Serves: 4

- 1/2 cup butter (1 stick)
- 1/2 cup brown sugar
- 2 tablespoons Worcestershire sauce
- 1 cup ketchup
- Salt and pepper to taste
- Juice and zest from 1 lemon

> **WINE PAIRING SUGGESTIONS:**
> *Waterville Winery Gewürztraminer*
> *Willow Crest Winery Riesling*

Melt the butter in a saucepan over medium heat. Add brown sugar, Worcestershire, ketchup, salt and pepper. Bring to a simmer and add lemon juice and zest.

Spread on salmon fillet and roast or grill, reserving some of the sauce to serve warm with the fish.

LEMON CRAB LINGUINE

Contributed by Executive Chef Daniel Carr and Chef de Cuisine Steve Coin, Visconti's Ristorante, page 110.

Prep time: 10 minutes
Cook time: 15 minutes
Serves: 2

- 2 cups linguine pasta, cooked al dente
- 1/3 cup unsalted butter
- Juice from 1 fresh lemon
- 3 teaspoons lemon zest, divided
- 1/8 teaspoon kosher salt
- 1/8 teaspoon ground black pepper
- 1 tablespoon fresh Italian parsley, chopped
- 1/2 cup heavy cream
- 1 cup Dungeness crabmeat

WINE PAIRING SUGGESTIONS:
Bella Terrazza Vineyards Estate Riesling

Crayelle Cellars Dry Riesling

Ryan Patrick Vineyards Reserve Chardonnay

Cook linguine pasta al dente according to the package directions.

Meanwhile, in a medium pan, melt butter over medium heat. Add lemon juice and 2 teaspoons lemon zest, salt, pepper and parsley. Bring to a simmer. Add cream and bring to boil.

After the sauce boils for about 30 seconds, add crab and turn off the heat. Add the last teaspoon of lemon zest and toss into the pasta.

LOBSTER MAC & CHEESE

Contributed by Kristen Wood, Icicle Ridge Winery, page 12.

Prep time: 20 minutes
Cook time: 40 minutes
Serves: 6

- 1 cup heavy cream
- 1 cup light cream
- 2 live OR pre-cooked lobsters
- 1 lb. elbow macaroni
- 2 tablespoons olive oil, divided
- 1 clove garlic, minced
- 2 large shallots, minced
- 1 cup dry white wine (Icicle Ridge Winery Sauvignon Blanc recommended)
- 1 tablespoon butter
- 2 tablespoons flour
- 1 cup Fontina cheese, grated
- 1 cup Gruyere cheese, grated
- Salt and pepper to taste

Garnish
- 1 cup fresh parsley, chopped

> **WINE PAIRING SUGGESTIONS:**
> *Boudreaux Cellars Chardonnay*
> *Icicle Ridge Sauvignon Blanc*
> *Silvara Vineyards Chardonnay*

Allow heavy and light cream to come to room temperature.

In an extra large stockpot, bring salted water to a boil to cook lobsters. In a regular stockpot, bring salted water to a boil for pasta.

Add live lobsters to large stockpot and cook for 12-14 minutes, or until shells have turned bright red. Remove lobsters from pot and allow to cool.

Add macaroni to the smaller pot and cook until al dente - timing will vary by pasta brand. Drain macaroni and toss with 1 tablespoon olive oil so it doesn't stick. Cover the pan to keep it warm.

When lobsters are cool enough to handle, use a lobster cracker to remove claw and tail meat, and chop into large chunks. Set aside.

Heat the remaining tablespoon of olive oil in a skillet over medium-high heat. Add garlic and shallots. Cook for 3 minutes. Add lobster meat and wine and simmer for 3-5 minutes. Remove from heat and set aside.

In a small saucepan, melt butter over medium-low heat. Slowly stir in flour to create a paste. Add heavy cream and light cream and stir into a paste, then bring to a simmer. Add the Fontina and Gruyere and stir until the sauce reaches a creamy consistency. Add salt and fresh ground pepper to taste.

Mix macaroni, lobster mixture, and cheese sauce in a large serving bowl, stirring well. Garnish with parsley and serve.

Mediterranean Rack of Lamb

**Contributed by Candace Egner,
'37 Cellars, page 5.**

Prep time: 25 minutes
Marinating time: 2-4 hours
Cook time: 12-24 minutes
Serves: 4-6

Wine Pairing Suggestions:
'37 Cellars Pepper Bridge Merlot
Crayelle Cellars Syrah
Stemilt Creek Winery Estate Syrah

- 2 racks of lamb (1-1/2 lbs. each)
- 4 cloves garlic
- 1 teaspoon coarse salt
- 1 small onion, peeled and cut in half lengthwise
- 1 teaspoon ground cumin
- 1 teaspoon ground coriander
- 1 teaspoon ground paprika
- 1 teaspoon ground white pepper
- 1/2 teaspoon ground cardamom
- 1 tablespoon ginger, freshly grated
- 2 teaspoons fresh rosemary, finely chopped
- 1/4 cup extra virgin olive oil
- 1 teaspoon coarse salt
- 1 teaspoon cumin
- Juice from 1/2 fresh lemon

French the racks of lamb or have your butcher do it for you by scraping all the fat and meat off between the bones. Trim all additional fat off each rack. Place racks in a baking dish.

Place the garlic and salt in a mixing bowl and mash to a smooth paste with the back of a wooden spoon. Coarsely grate the onion into the bowl. Stir in cumin, coriander, paprika, white pepper, cardamom, ginger, rosemary and oil. Spread the spice paste over the meaty parts, but not on the rib bones. Let lamb marinate in the refrigerator, covered, for 2-4 hours. Before cooking, remove from the refrigerator and let sit at room temperature for 15 minutes.

Preheat grill to medium-high. Cover the bare bones with aluminum foil and remove halfway through cooking so rib bones can brown nicely, otherwise they WILL burn. Place the lamb on the hot grate, meat side down, and grill until cooked to taste (about 6 minutes per side for medium rare) and at least 145°F on an instant-read meat thermometer (cooking time will depend on the size of the racks.) Stand the racks upright for a minute to grill each end. You'll probably get flare-ups so be ready to move the lamb around as needed.

Alternatively, you can broil the lamb in the oven on high for about 12 minutes per side.

Transfer the racks to a platter and let rest for 3 minutes. Carve into chops. Sprinkle with a mixture of coarse salt and cumin and a squeeze of fresh lemon.

Mole de Oaxaca

Contributed by Cappy Bond & Price Gledhill, South Restaurant, page 110.

Mole (moe-LAY) is a rich Mexican sauce, usually served on chicken over rice.

Prep time: 30 minutes
Cook time: 45 minutes
Serves: 6-8

> **WINE PAIRING SUGGESTIONS:**
> *'37 Cellars Pepper Bridge Merlot*
> *Eagle Creek Winery Merlot*

- 5 ancho chilies (dried)
- 10 pasilla chilies (dried)
- 15 guajillo chilies (dried)
- 1/2 cup olive oil, divided
- 1/4 cup raisins
- 1/4 cup almonds
- 1/4 cup sesame seeds
- 1/4 teaspoon ground cloves
- 1/2 stick cinnamon
- 2 cloves garlic, chopped
- 1 piece Mexican egg bread, torn into pieces
- 1 plantain, or banana, sliced
- 2 tomatoes, cut in half
- 4-1/4 cups chicken broth, divided
- 1/2 cup Mexican chocolate, chopped
- 1 lb. boneless chicken breasts, grilled or broiled

Clean the outside of the chilies with a damp cloth. Use scissors to cut off the stems and cut up the side of the chilies to remove the seeds and veins.

Heat 1/4 cup olive oil in a pan and fry the chilies until they begin to darken and become crispy. Place them in a bowl lined with paper towels.

In the same pan, heat the raisins until they puff up and start to brown. Remove them from the pan. Add the almonds and fry until they start to brown. Add the sesame seeds, ground clove, cinnamon, and garlic and cook until the almonds are a dark brown. Remove from the pan. Add the bread and fry until the remaining oil has been absorbed; remove from pan. Add 1/4 cup more oil and fry the plantain until golden brown.

In a separate dry pan, roast the tomato halves on medium heat until they start to brown. Combine the raisins, almond mixture, bread, plantain and tomatoes in a blender with 1 cup chicken broth and blend until smooth. Transfer to a bowl.

Puree the fried chilies in the blender with 1-1/2 cups chicken broth until smooth.

Pour any remaining oil from the pan into a deep pot and add the chili paste. Cook on medium heat, stirring constantly, for about 3 minutes. Add the nut and spice mixture and stir for 3 more minutes. Add chocolate and stir until melted, about 5 minutes. Add additional chicken broth and cook for another 5 minutes or until the mole starts to bubble. Season with salt to taste and serve over chicken.

Mushroom Artichoke Chicken

Contributed by Pamela Kiehn, Beecher Hill House, page 107.

Prep time: 5 minutes
Cook time: 36 minutes
Serves: 4

- 14 oz. jar artichokes in oil
- 4 boneless skinless chicken breasts
- 1/4 teaspoon salt
- 1/4 teaspoon pepper
- 3/4 cup mushrooms, sliced
- 3 garlic cloves, sliced
- 1/2 cup white wine
- 6 tablespoons butter
- Flat leaf parsley, chopped

Wine Pairing Suggestions:
Ryan Patrick Vineyards Naked Chardonnay

Waterville Winery Riesling

Wine Tip:
Artichokes make all wines taste sweet. Pair artichoke dishes with bone-dry wines.

Drain oil from artichoke jar into a sauté pan, reserving the artichokes. Generously salt and pepper the chicken breasts and sauté them in the artichoke oil over medium heat, browning both sides.

Remove to a plate and keep warm. Add mushrooms and garlic to the oil in pan and cook until mushrooms release their liquid. Add the wine and simmer, scraping up all the bits from bottom of the pan to deglaze. Add in the artichokes and bring to a simmer.

Return the chicken to the pan, cover and simmer on low until the chicken is done, about 5 minutes. Remove from heat, stir in butter until melted and add the parsley.

Mushroom Risotto

**Contributed by Dave Hambleton,
The Cheesemonger's Shop, page 107.**

This is a rich dish that can be a main course, or a featured side with a steak. Risotto is a type of rice that comes out creamy and almost pasta-like. The earthy mushroom flavor is really enhanced with a little bit of thyme.

WINE PAIRING SUGGESTIONS:
Bella Terrazza Vineyards Estate Bella Rosso
La Toscana Winery Rosso Toscano
La Toscana Winery Cabernet Sauvignon Cabernet Franc blend

Prep time: 20 minutes
Cook time: 30 minutes
Serves: 3-5

- 6 cups chicken broth
- 3 tablespoons olive oil, divided
- 2 lbs. mushrooms, thinly sliced (portabella, white button, cremini, etc.)
- 2 shallots, diced
- 1/4 teaspoon thyme
- 1-1/2 cups Arborio rice (no substitutions)
- 1/2 cup dry white wine
- 4 tablespoons butter
- 3 tablespoons chives, finely chopped
- 1/3 cup Pecorino Romano cheese, freshly grated
- Sea salt to taste
- Freshly ground black pepper to taste

Warm chicken broth in a saucepan over low heat. Have a ladle handy for transferring to the risotto pot.

Meanwhile, heat 2 tablespoons olive oil in a large saucepan. Sauté mushrooms, shallots and thyme for about 3 minutes or until soft. Set the mushrooms aside on a plate until the rice is almost done.

Add rice and remaining tablespoon of the olive oil to the saucepan. Stir to coat with oil. Cook over medium heat for about 3 minutes. When the rice has taken on a pale golden color, pour in wine, stirring constantly until fully absorbed.

Ladle in about 1/2 cup of the warm broth into the rice and stir until it is absorbed. Repeat this process until you have used all the broth.
When the liquid is completely absorbed, the rice should have a creamy texture. If it is still too al dente for your taste, you can continue the process with water until the texture is right.

Remove from heat, and stir in mushrooms with their liquid, butter, chives, and Pecorino Romano. Season with salt and pepper to taste.

To reheat leftovers, add 1/4 cup water and slowly heat in a saucepan.

Red Wine Cherry Pork

Contributed by Joanne Saliby,
Wenatchee World *Living Well* blog, page 109.

Prep time: 25 minutes
Marinate time: 1 hour
Cook time: 30 minutes
Serves: 4-6

> **WINE PAIRING SUGGESTIONS:**
> Bella Terrazza Vineyards Estate Cabernet Franc
> Horan Estates HVH Red Blend
> Wedge Mountain Winery Lemberger (Semi-Sweet)

- 2 tablespoons + 2 teaspoons grapeseed oil, divided
- 1 teaspoon lemon zest
- 1/4 teaspoon thyme
- 1-1/2 lbs. pork tenderloin, trimmed of silver skin
- Salt and pepper
- 1 cup brown jasmine rice
- 1/4 cup onion OR shallots, finely diced
- 2 cloves garlic, minced
- 1-1/2 cups dry red wine
- Sprig of fresh thyme
- 1/2 cup low sodium chicken broth
- 1/2 cup mushroom or vegetable broth
- 1/4 cup dried tart cherries, finely chopped
- 4 tablespoons cold unsalted butter, cut into 1/2 inch pieces
- 1/2 teaspoon kosher salt
- 1-2 grinds black pepper

Combine 1 tablespoon grapeseed oil, lemon zest, thyme and salt and pepper. Rub pork with the mixture and let rest in the refrigerator for 1 hour.

Preheat oven to 350°F. Start the rice about 15 minutes before beginning to cook the pork and cook according to package directions.

Heat a medium sauté pan on the stove over medium-high heat. Add 1 tablespoon oil. When the oil is hot, place the pork in pan and lower heat to medium. Brown the pork on all sides. Remove and place in small ovenproof dish. Bake the pork until the temperature reads 155°F. Remove, cover and let rest for 10 minutes.

Remove and save drippings from the pork. In the same pan, heat 2 teaspoons grapeseed oil, onion and garlic on medium heat until softened. Add wine. Reduce to 3/4 cup. Add thyme, drippings, chicken and mushroom broth and cherries.

Simmer until reduced to 1-1/4 cups. Remove thyme sprig. Remove from heat. Whisk in butter a few pieces at a time until fully incorporated. Add salt and pepper. Slice the pork into 1/4 inch pieces and serve over rice, drizzled in sauce.

Recipe Tip
As a general rule, it takes 20 minutes per pound to cook pork tenderloin at 350°F. Use a meat thermometer for best results.

Roast Pork Loin with Bartlett Pear Sauce

Contributed by Pamela Kiehn, Beecher Hill House, page 107.

Prep time: 15 minutes
Cook time: 1-2 hours
Serves: 6-8

Wine Pairing Suggestions:
Boudreaux Cellars Riesling
Cascadia Winery Apple Wine
Silvara Vineyards Riesling

Pork
- 1/4 cup olive oil
- 1/4 cup Dijon mustard
- 1/4 cup honey
- 1 teaspoon kosher salt
- 1/2 teaspoon pepper
- 3 to 4 lb. pork loin roast

Sauce
- 1 cup butter (2 sticks), divided
- 1/2 cup carrot, finely grated (about 1 medium carrot)
- 1 large sweet onion
- 2 cups chicken stock
- 2 cups beef stock
- 1/8 cup Worcestershire sauce
- 3 to 4 firm but ripe pears (Bartlett pears recommended), divided
- 1 tablespoon lemon juice
- Salt and pepper to taste
- 1/4 cup flour

Preheat oven to 350°F. Mix olive oil, mustard, honey, salt and pepper and rub onto the roast. Bake until the meat reaches 155°F, about 1-1.5 hours; about 25 minutes per pound of pork loin.

Sprinkle the peeled and diced pears with lemon juice to prevent them from browning; set aside.

About 45 minutes before the roast is done, melt one stick of butter in a large sauté pan to start the sauce. Sauté carrot and onion over medium-high heat until soft – about 5 minutes. Add chicken and beef stock, Worcestershire and about one pear. Simmer until sauce is reduced by half, about 30 minutes.

When the roast is done, remove from oven and let rest.

Pour the juices into your sauce and add salt and pepper to taste. In a separate pan, melt 1 stick of butter. Slowly stir in flour to create a roux. Once it starts to turn golden brown, add the roux to the saucepan and simmer until it thickens. Stir the pears into the sauce and heat through.

Slice pork roast and serve drizzled with sauce.

Saffron Quail

Contributed by Rob Newsom, Boudreaux Cellars, page 7.

Prep time: 30 minutes
Cook time: 1 hour 15 minutes
Serves: 4-6

> **WINE PAIRING SUGGESTIONS:**
> *Boudreaux Cellars Reserve Cabernet Sauvignon*
> *Boudreaux Cellars Syrah*

- Clay baking dish
- 4 quail OR 1 large pheasant, OR 2 grouse, quartered
- 2 tablespoons olive oil
- 1/2 teaspoon sea salt
- 1/2 teaspoon black pepper
- 8 cloves garlic, chopped
- 2 cups green onions, chopped into 1 inch long pieces, including roots
- 2 cups carrots, sliced
- 1/4 cup butter (1/2 stick)
- 1.7 grams or more saffron
- 1/2 teaspoon dried rosemary
- 1 package angel hair pasta, cooked according to package directions
- French baguette bread

Preheat oven to 350°F. Soak a clay baking dish in water for 15-30 minutes.

Brown quail in a cast iron skillet with oil, salt and pepper for about 4 minutes each side. If the meat starts to stick, scrape the bottom of the pan with a spatula. Add garlic, green onions and carrots and sauté with the quail for about 5 minutes. Add butter and stir until melted. Remove from heat.

Pour the contents of skillet into the clay baking dish. Sprinkle with saffron and rosemary and mix slightly. Cover and bake for at least an hour, stirring once after 30 minutes. It is ready when the meat is falling off the bone and the contents of the dish are a glazed brown color.

Prepare angel hair pasta according to package directions. Drain. Briefly reheat the cast iron skillet and add the angel hair pasta, stirring to coat with the leftover seasonings from browning the quail.

Place the pasta in a bowl and spoon quail over top, including plenty of broth. Serve with French bread. Don't be afraid to eat the quail with your fingers.

Recipe Tips
- *You can use a casserole dish instead of a clay baking dish, but the quail will cook more evenly in clay.*
- *The more carrots you add, the sweeter the dish will be.*

Salmon in Balsamic Blackberry Wine Sauce

Contributed by Marlies Egberding, The Savory Table, page 110.

Prep time: 10 minutes
Cook time: 20 minutes
Serves: 2

- 1 small onion, minced
- 1 clove garlic, diced
- 1 tablespoon butter
- 1 tablespoon fresh rosemary, chopped
- 1 cup balsamic vinegar
- 2 cups blackberry wine (Pasek Cellars Blackberry Wine recommended)
- 2 fillets salmon

> **Wine Pairing Suggestions:**
> Wedge Mountain Winery Lemberger (Semi-Sweet)
>
> **Wine Tip:**
> Offset this slightly sweet sauce with a drier wine. Salmon, an oily fish, can handle a red wine. Most white fish, however, should be paired with white wine.

Sauté onion and garlic in butter on medium-high heat until the onions are translucent and slightly browned, about 5 minutes.

Add rosemary, balsamic vinegar and blackberry wine and simmer on medium heat, stirring often. Simmer sauce until it has reduced to about 1 cup.

Place salmon skin side down on a broiling pan. Broil on low with the oven door open for about 10 minutes for every inch of fillet thickness. It is done when it can be easily flaked with a fork.

Serve sauce warm over salmon.

Recipe Tip
Allow the sauce to cool completely and use as a delicious salad dressing!

Scalloped Oysters

**Contributed by Julie Moyles,
La Toscana Winery, page 13.**

"My mother got this recipe from her mother and served it frequently during the summer when they lived in their beach cabin near Olympia, WA, where the fresh oyster supply was nearly limitless." – Julie Moyles

> **WINE PAIRING SUGGESTIONS:**
> *Bella Terrazza Vineyards Estate Chardonnay*
> *Icicle Ridge Winery Chardonnay*
> *Waterville Winery NOaked Chardonnay*

Prep time: 20 minutes
Cook time: 45 minutes
Serves: 8

- 1 pint oysters
- 2-1/2 cups Saltine crackers (1 sleeve)
- 1/2 cup butter, melted (1 stick)
- Fresh ground black pepper
- 1/2 cup light cream
- 1/2 teaspoon salt
- 1/2 teaspoon Worcestershire sauce
- 1/4 teaspoon Tabasco
- 1/4 teaspoon garlic powder

Preheat oven to 350°F. Grease a 9x9 inch casserole dish.

Drain the oysters, saving the liquid for later use. Cut the oysters in half, unless they are quite small.

Crush the crackers into crumbs and toss with melted butter. Spread a third of the cracker mixture into the bottom of the casserole dish. Cover with half of the oysters and grind black pepper over the top.

Layer another third of the cracker crumbs, followed by the last of the oysters, more pepper, and finally, the last third of the crackers.

Combine the saved oyster liquid with light cream to make a total of 1 cup. Add salt, Worcestershire sauce, Tabasco and garlic powder, adjusting seasonings to taste as needed.

Pour the mixture evenly over the assembled casserole. Bake for 45 minutes. Serve as a side dish or with a salad or fresh fruit.

Recipe Tip
To reduce the amount of sodium in the dish, omit the salt from the recipe and use unsalted crackers and butter.

Shrimp Étouffée

**Contributed by Rob Newsom,
Boudreaux Cellars, page 7.**

Prep time: 40 minutes
Cook time: 1 hour 15 minutes
Serves: 4-6

- 2 to 3 lbs. peeled shrimp, shells reserved
- 8 cups water
- 2 teaspoons salt
- 1 teaspoon cayenne pepper
- 1/2 teaspoon white pepper
- 1/2 teaspoon black pepper
- 1 teaspoon dried basil
- 1/2 teaspoon dried thyme
- 1/4 cup canola oil
- 1/4 cup flour
- 1-1/2 cups yellow onion, diced
- 5 large garlic cloves, diced
- 3 celery stalks, diced
- 1/2 green or red bell pepper, diced
- 1/2 cup butter (1 stick)
- 1 cup white rice
- 1 cup green onions (about 2 bunches), diced
- French bread

> **WINE PAIRING SUGGESTIONS:**
> *Boudreaux Cellars Chardonnay*
> *Boudreaux Cellars Riesling*
> *Eagle Creek Winery Gewürztraminer*
>
> **WINE TIP:**
> *Balance out spicy dishes with sweet wines.*

Peel the shrimp, rinse them, and refrigerate. Place the shrimp shells in 8 cups water over high heat and simmer the stock down to 4 cups – about 1 hour.

To create the seasoning, combine the salt, cayenne, white and black pepper, basil and thyme in a small bowl. Set aside.

When ready, use 2 cups of shrimp stock for the water to make the rice according to package directions.

Meanwhile, warm a cast-iron skillet on medium-high heat and add the canola oil. Slowly sprinkle in the flour, stirring constantly with a spatula until you have slowly turned the flour to a dark brown color. If you burn the roux, it will quickly turn black and you will have to discard it and start over. Stir in the onion, garlic, celery and bell pepper and sauté for 3-4 minutes. Add 1 tablespoon of the seasoning and stir well. Stir in 2 cups of shrimp stock and bring to a simmer. Add butter and stir until melted.

Five minutes before the rice is done, add the shrimp, green onions, and the remaining seasoning to the other vegetables and stir until the shrimp turn pink.

Serve over rice with French bread to sop up the extra broth.

Spaghetti with Merlot Tomato Sauce

Contributed by Alan Yanagimachi, Cascadia Winery, page 8.

Prep time: 5 minutes
Cook time: 20 minutes
Serves: 4-6

- 1 lb. ground meat OR Italian sausage
- 3 cloves garlic, diced
- 1-1/2 tablespoons Italian seasoning
- Salt and pepper to taste
- 24 oz. can tomato sauce
- 28 oz. can crushed tomatoes
- 1/4 cup tomato paste
- 1/4 cup brown sugar
- 3/4 cup Merlot (Cascadia Winery Merlot recommended)
- 1 lb. package spaghetti noodles
- French bread

*<u>**Wine Pairing Suggestions:**</u>*
Cascadia Winery Merlot
La Toscana Rosso Toscano

Brown the meat with garlic, Italian seasoning, salt and pepper to taste. Drain off the fat. Add the tomato sauce, crushed tomatoes, tomato paste, brown sugar and wine and simmer on medium heat, stirring occasionally.

Cook the spaghetti noodles according to package directions. By the time the noodles are done the sauce is ready.

Serve sauce over spaghetti noodles with French bread.

<u>*Recipe Tip:*</u>
The complex Merlot flavors and the brown sugar really soften the tomato flavor, making it appear as if you've been simmering the sauce for hours.

Sweet and Spicy Black Beans

Contributed by Traci Hartmann, Bella Terrazza Vineyards, page 6.

Prep time: 15 minutes
Cook time: 25 minutes
Serves: 12

- 2 tablespoons olive oil
- 2 medium onions, chopped
- 2 cloves garlic, minced
- 2-4 jalapeño peppers, chopped with seeds
- 4 15 oz. cans black beans, drained
- 28 oz. can diced tomatoes with basil, garlic and oregano, drained
- 1/3 cup honey
- 1/3 cup brown sugar, packed
- 2 tablespoons apple cider vinegar
- 1 teaspoon salt
- 1 teaspoon ginger powder (optional)

Wine Pairing Suggestions:

Bella Terrazza Vineyards Estate Pinot Grigio

Waterville Winery NOaked Chardonnay

Willow Crest Winery Riesling

Wine Tip:

Balance out spicy dishes with sweet wines.

Heat oil in a large pot over medium-high heat. Add onions, garlic and peppers and sauté until almost tender, about 5-7 minutes.

Add the beans, diced tomatoes, honey, brown sugar, vinegar, salt and ginger. Cook until heated through, about 15 minutes.

Serve with chips and salsa or as a side dish to any Mexican meal.

Recipe Tip:
To reduce the spiciness, remove the seeds from the jalapeño before using.

Thai Cashew Chicken

**Contributed by Traci Hartmann,
Bella Terrazza Vineyards, page 6.**

Prep time: 10 minutes
Cook time: 20 minutes
Serves: 4

- 2 cups rice
- 3 tablespoons olive oil, divided
- 1 lb. boneless skinless chicken breasts, cut into strips
- 1/4 teaspoon salt
- 1/4 teaspoon pepper
- 1/4 teaspoon garlic salt
- 2-1/2 tablespoons Thai chili paste
- 1/2 cup low-sodium chicken broth
- 1 large red bell pepper, seeded and cut into 1/2 inch pieces
- 1/2 large onion, cut into 1/2 inch pieces
- 1/4 cup oyster sauce
- 1 tablespoon sugar
- 4 dried red chilies (arbol chilies recommended - HOT)
- 1/2 cup dry roasted, unsalted cashews
- 10 green onions, cut into 1 inch pieces
- Juice from 1 lime (about 1 tablespoon)

Wine Pairing Suggestions:
Bella Terrazza Vineyard Estate Gewürztraminer

Bella Terrazza Vineyard Estate Riesling

Boudreaux Cellars Riesling

Prepare rice according to package directions.

Heat 2 tablespoons olive oil in a large skillet over medium-high heat. Add the chicken, season with salt, pepper and garlic salt and stir fry until cooked through, about 7-9 minutes. Remove from pan and set aside.

Add 1 tablespoon oil to the empty skillet on medium-high heat. Add the chili paste, stirring to break it up. Add the chicken broth, red bell pepper, onion, oyster sauce and sugar, stirring well until fully incorporated. Simmer for about 3 minutes.

Lower the heat to medium, return the chicken to the skillet and cook until the sauce is slightly thickened and the vegetables are tender, about 4-5 minutes. Add the chilies, cashews and green onions.

Stir to combine, squeeze lime juice over top and serve immediately over rice.

Recipe Tip:
To reduce the spiciness, use fewer red chilies or cut them out completely.

ENTRÉES

THAI COCONUT BOUILLABAISSE

**Contributed by Danielle Mitrakul,
Crayelle Cellars, page 9.**

"I was introduced to Thai food when I was dating my husband, whose father is from Thailand. My Father-In-Law always enjoys an Italian cioppino and a French bouillabaisse. This recipe, originally developed for Cooking Light Magazine *by Laura Zapalowski, is a complementary blend of both Thai and French cuisines."* – Danielle Mitrakul

WINE PAIRING SUGGESTIONS:
Crayelle Cellars Dry Riesling
Wedge Mountain Winery Dry Riesling

Prep time: 15 Minutes
Cook time: 50 Minutes
Serves: 6

Stock
- 1 lb. jumbo shrimp, peeled and deveined, shells reserved
- 2 tablespoons olive oil
- 1/2 cup celery, chopped
- 1/2 cup carrots, chopped
- 1/2 cup onion, chopped
- 2-1/2 cups cold water
- 3 black peppercorns
- 1 bay leaf

Bouillabaisse
- 1 teaspoon olive oil
- 1/2 cup celery, chopped
- 1/2 cup carrots, chopped
- 1/2 cup onion, chopped
- 1 red bell pepper, chopped
- 1 tomato, chopped
- 1 tablespoon fresh garlic, minced
- 1 teaspoon red curry paste
- 4 Kaffir lime leaves, or zest from 2 limes
- 14 oz. can coconut milk
- 12 clams, scrubbed
- 12 mussels, scrubbed and debearded
- 1/4 cup fresh basil, chopped
- 1/4 cup fresh cilantro, chopped
- 1 teaspoon salt
- 1/4 teaspoon black pepper
- 1 skinned halibut or other white fish fillet, cut into 1 inch pieces

Garnish
- Lime wedges

continued on page 85

Thai Coconut Bouillabaisse (continued)

continued from page 84

Peel the shrimp, rinse and refrigerate.

Heat a saucepan over medium-high heat. Add olive oil and shrimp shells to pan. Stir for 3-5 minutes. Stir in celery, carrots, and onion. Cook for about 1 minute.

Add water, peppercorns, and bay leaf and bring to a boil. Reduce to a medium-low heat and simmer for about 30 minutes, stirring occasionally. Strain the broth and discard the shrimp shells and vegetables.

To make the bouillabaisse, heat oil in a large saucepan over medium heat. Add celery, carrots and onion and cook for 3-5 minutes. Add bell pepper. Stir in tomato, garlic, curry paste, and lime leaves or zest. Cook for 2 minutes, stirring constantly.

Stir in the shrimp stock and coconut milk and bring to a boil. Add clams and mussels. Cover, reduce heat to low, and cook for 2 minutes or until clams and mussels open.

Remove pan from stove and discard any unopened shells. Stir in shrimp, basil, cilantro, salt, pepper and halibut.

Cover the pan and let stand 5 minutes, or until shrimp and halibut are done. You should be able to easily flake the halibut with a fork. Discard the lime rind. Distribute evenly into bowls. Garnish with lime wedges and add salt and pepper to taste.

TUSCAN CABBAGE & MUSHROOMS

**Contributed by Julie Moyles,
La Toscana Winery, page 13.**

Prep time: 25 minutes
Cook time: 30 minutes
Serves: 2-4

> **WINE PAIRING SUGGESTIONS:**
> *La Toscana Winery Lemberger*
> *Waterville Winery Temperanillo*
> *Wedge Mountain Winery Chardonnay*

- 2 medium leeks, sliced
- 3 teaspoons butter, divided
- 1 oz. pancetta OR 3 slices bacon
- 2 cloves garlic, diced
- Salt and pepper to taste
- 1 cup chicken broth, divided
- 1 head Savoy cabbage, thinly sliced
- 1 cup Shiitake mushrooms, whole with stems removed

Cut the white soft part off the leeks and discard the green stalks. Cut in half lengthwise and rinse well. Cut crosswise into thin slices; rinse again and drain in a colander.

Melt 2 teaspoons butter in large skillet over medium-high heat. Add pancetta and sauté lightly. If using bacon, cook until crisp. Drain the pancetta or bacon on paper towels and cut into small pieces.

Lower heat to medium. Stir in the remaining 1 teaspoon butter, leeks and garlic. Season with salt and pepper and add 1/4 cup chicken broth. Simmer on medium heat, uncovered, until tender.

Add cabbage and 1/4 cup more chicken broth. Cover and simmer on medium-low until tender, checking every 5 minutes to make sure it's not drying out. If there appears to be little liquid left, add more chicken broth, 1/4 cup at a time. After the cabbage is tender – about 15 minutes – stir in the mushrooms, replace the lid and simmer for 5-7 more minutes. Add more salt and pepper to taste.

Sprinkle with pancetta or bacon before serving.

"Snow Grapes" by Kerry Siderius

"Vineyard and Lupine" by Kerry Siderius

Audrey's Apple Pie

Contributed by Morgan Fraser,
Savoring Leavenworth **author, page 120.**

"My grandmother grew up in Cowiche, WA, outside of Yakima. Audrey (Nana) was an amazing cook but an even better baker; she was probably making this pie from the local apples since she was very young. More than 15 years after Nana's death, the whole family still talks about the magic she created in the kitchen. We use her pie recipes at Thanksgiving and Christmas and when Golden Delicious apples are harvested in September and October."
– Morgan Fraser

Prep time: 30 minutes
Cook time: 1 hour 15 minutes
Serves: 8

> **WINE PAIRING SUGGESTION:**
> *Swakane Winery Estate Late Harvest Riesling*

- 2 single uncooked pie crusts (see Audrey's Pie Crust recipe on page 90)
- 5 large Golden Delicious apples, cored, peeled and sliced
- 1 cup sugar + 1 teaspoon sugar, divided
- 1 teaspoon cinnamon
- 3 tablespoons butter
- 1 tablespoon milk

Garnish
- Vanilla ice cream or sharp cheddar cheese

Preheat oven to 425°F. Carefully place an uncooked pie crust in a 9 inch pie pan and fill the pan with the sliced apples. Sprinkle cinnamon and 1 cup sugar over the apples. Divide the butter into 10 small pieces and place them on top of the apple mixture. Roll out the second crust and place it over the apples. Seal the edges with your fingers or a fork. Cut off all but about a 3/4 inch of dough around the edges.

Cut diagonal slits in top crust for venting during cooking. Brush the top of the pie with milk and sprinkle with a little sugar.

Bake for 15 minutes at 425°F. Lower the temperature to 350°F and bake for 1 hour or until top is golden brown.

Serve the pie hot with vanilla ice cream, whipped cream or topped with a slice of cheese.

DESSERTS

Audrey's Pie Crust

Contributed by Morgan Fraser,
Savoring Leavenworth author, page 120.

This is the crust recipe that goes with Audrey's Apple Pie on page 91. Pre-bake the crust for custard-filled pies or fill and bake for fruit pies. You can also make the dough in advance and refrigerate it.

Prep time: 45 minutes
Set time: 45 minutes to 12 hours
Cook time: 30 minutes (optional)
Makes: 2 single crusts

- 2-1/3 cups all-purpose flour
- 1 teaspoon salt
- 1 cup shortening OR butter
- 1 egg
- 1-1/2 teaspoons cider vinegar
- 1/4 cup cold water

> **WINE TIP:**
> *Pair the crust according to the filling. Typically a wine should be sweeter than the food it's paired with. Pies pear best with an ice wine or dessert wine.*

Combine the flour, salt and shortening or butter in a large bowl. Blend with a pastry blender, pastry cutter or knives until crumbly.

In a small bowl, whisk together the egg, cider vinegar and water. Drizzle over the flour mixture and mix thoroughly. The dough will be soft and a little sticky. If it's too sticky, add a little more flour.

Shape the dough into two patties, wrap in plastic wrap and place in the freezer for 45 minutes, or in the refrigerator overnight.

Unbaked crust
When chilled, take one patty out of the refrigerator and roll out on a floured surface until it's slightly bigger than the pie pan. Repeat with the second crust.

Fill the crust with filling and bake according to pie recipe directions.

Pre-baked crust
Preheat the oven to 350°F. Press the crust firmly into the pie pan and freeze the crust until chilled, or at least 30 minutes to keep the crust from slipping down the sides of the pan.

When the pie crust is chilled, line it with parchment paper, wax paper or aluminum foil. Fill the crust at least two-thirds full with weights: dry beans, rice, or stainless-steel pie weights. Bake with the weights for 20 minutes. Remove from the oven, cool for a few minutes and carefully remove pie weights. Poke holes in the bottom of the pie crust with a fork and bake for an additional 10 minutes without the weights until the crust is golden brown. Cool completely before filling. You can cover the edges of the pie with aluminum foil during baking to keep the edges from drying out or burning.

Recipe Tip
- *The amount of water used may vary with elevation and humidity.*
- *Use butter instead of shortening for a healthier yet still delicious crust.*

Caramel Sauce with Apple Wine

**Contributed by Alan Yanagimachi,
Cascadia Winery, page 8.**

Cook time: 8-10 minutes
Serves: 4-6

- 1 cup sugar
- 4 tablespoons warmed apple wine (Cascadia Winery Apple Wine recommended)
- 1-1/2 tablespoons heavy cream

Heat sugar on medium high heat, stirring constantly, until it becomes a golden brown liquid. Carefully add the warmed apple wine, but be careful, the sugar will bubble!

Continue to stir until the sugar and wine are incorporated. Stir in heavy cream and remove from heat. Allow to cool slightly to thicken and serve over pie, ice cream, bread pudding or your favorite dessert.

> **WINE TIP:**
> Pair the sauce according what it's topping. Typically a wine should be sweeter than the food it's paired with. Desserts pair best with an ice wine or dessert wine.

Grandma Judy's Sour Cream Pear Pie

Contributed by Kristen Wood, Icicle Ridge Winery, page 12.

"This pie is a Wagoner favorite all year long, but especially enjoyed in the fall, right after all our pears are safely off the trees. If Grandma doesn't bring a pear pie to family gatherings, we are all a little disappointed." – Kristen Wood

Prep time: 20 minutes
Cook time: 50 minutes
Serves: 6-8

> **Wine Pairing Suggestions:**
> *Icicle Ridge Winery Ice Riesling*
> *Swakane Winery Estate Late Harvest Riesling*

- 1 unbaked 9 inch pie shell (see Audrey's Pie Crust recipe on page 90)

Filling
- 1 tablespoon lemon juice
- 1 cup sour cream
- 1 egg
- 3/4 cup sugar
- 1 teaspoon vanilla
- 1/4 teaspoon salt
- 2 tablespoons flour
- 4 ripe pears, peeled and diced

Pecan Streusel Topping
- 1/4 cup flour
- 1/4 cup brown sugar
- 1 teaspoon cinnamon
- 1/4 cup butter, cut in small pieces (1/2 stick)
- 1/4 cup pecans, finely chopped

Preheat oven to 375°F. Dice the pears and sprinkle them with lemon juice to keep them from browning. Set aside. Blend the sour cream, egg, sugar, vanilla, salt and flour until smooth. Fold in the diced pears and pour into the pie shell. Bake for 40 minutes.

To create the topping, combine flour, brown sugar and cinnamon. Cut in the butter with a pastry cutter or knife before adding the pecans.

Sprinkle the topping over the pie and bake another 10 minutes. Let cool for about 10 minutes and serve.

La Toscana Apple Coffee Cake

**Contributed by Julie Moyles,
La Toscana Winery, page 13.**

This longtime family favorite, served with scrambled eggs and fresh fruit compote, makes a festive and delectable special occasion brunch.

Prep time: 25 minutes
Cook time: 45-50 minutes
Serves: 8

- 1/2 cup flour
- 1/2 cup white sugar
- 1/2 cup brown sugar
- 1/2 teaspoon cinnamon
- 1/8 teaspoon salt
- 1/2 cup cold butter, cut into small pieces (1 stick) + 1 tablespoon, divided
- 1 egg
- 1/2 cup buttermilk
- 1 teaspoon soda
- 2 large Fuji apples, peeled, cored and thinly sliced
- 1/4 teaspoon cinnamon

WINE PAIRING SUGGESTIONS:
*La Toscana Winery
Annika's Riesling*

Preheat the oven to 350°F. In a large bowl, blend flour, white and brown sugar, cinnamon and salt. Cut in the butter. Use your hands or a pastry cutter to combine the mixture until it resembles coarse crumbs.

Divide the mixture into two equal parts of about two cups each. Combine the egg, buttermilk and baking soda and stir into one part. Pour this batter into a 10 inch greased pie dish. Arrange the apple slices over the top, and cover with the remaining crumbs. Sprinkle the top with cinnamon and dot with butter.

Bake for 45-50 minutes, or until a toothpick inserted in the coffeecake comes out clean.

DESSERTS

Mango Raspberry Cobbler

Contributed by Julie Moyles, La Toscana Winery, page 13.

Prep time: 20 minutes
Cook time: 25 minutes
Serves: 6

> **Wine Pairing Suggestions:**
>
> *Pasek Cellars Raspberry Dessert Wine*
>
> *Wedge Mountain Winery Roses & Rubies*

Filling
- 3 tablespoons flour
- 1/4 teaspoon ground ginger
- 1/8 teaspoon cardamom
- 1/8 teaspoon cinnamon
- 1/8 teaspoon ground nutmeg
- 1/3 cup packed brown sugar
- 4 cups fresh raspberries
- 3 cups mango, chopped (about 2 large mangoes)
- 1/2 teaspoon vanilla

Topping
- 3/4 cup oats (not instant)
- 1/2 cup flour
- 1/2 cup packed brown sugar
- 1/2 tsp cinnamon
- 1/4 cup butter, cut into small pieces (1/2 stick) + 2 tablespoons butter, cut into small pieces (divided)

Preheat oven to 400°F. Mix flour, ginger, cardamom, cinnamon, nutmeg and brown sugar. Gently combine with raspberries, mango and vanilla. Spoon into a greased 7x11 inch baking dish.

For the topping, combine the oats, flour, brown sugar and cinnamon. Using your hands or a pastry cutter, mix in the butter until the topping resembles coarse crumbs. Sprinkle the topping evenly over the filling and dot with remaining butter.

Bake for 25 minutes. Serve hot with vanilla ice cream.

Recipe Tip
Try using blackberries or a mix of blackberries and raspberries, or fresh peaches instead of mangoes, for a change in flavor and texture.

RASPBERRY CHEESECAKE SAUCE

Contributed by Marlies Egberding, The Savory Table, page 109.

Prep time: 3 minutes
Cook time: 30 minutes
Chill time: 1-2 hours
Serves: 4

WINE PAIRING SUGGESTIONS:
Pasek Cellars Muscat Canelli
Pasek Cellars Raspberry Dessert Wine
Wedge Mountain Winery Roses & Rubies

- 1 bottle raspberry dessert wine (Pasek Cellars Raspberry Dessert Wine recommended)
- 1 tablespoon sugar
- 1 tablespoon cornstarch
- 2 tablespoons cold water
- 2 cups raspberries

In a saucepan, combine wine and sugar and boil, uncovered, over medium-high heat until reduced by half, about 30 minutes.

In a small glass or bowl, mix cornstarch with cold water until the cornstarch is completely dissolved. Slowly stir the mixture into the simmering wine and continue to stir for about 1 minute. Remove from heat and allow to cool for about 10 minutes.

Fold in the raspberries and chill completely. Serve over your favorite cheesecake, ice cream or dessert.

Recipe Tips
- *Try substituting another dessert wine for the raspberry wine, or change out the raspberries for blackberries or blueberries.*
- *Use this sauce to top ice cream, cake or fruit.*

ORCHARD PEAR TART

Contributed by Executive Chef Thomas Obregon, Mountain Home Lodge, page 109.

"Our valley offers an abundant selection of sun ripened orchard fruit. Many requests are made by our guests for our Orchard Pear Tart. Dennis and Nancy Nicholson's Orchard located just a few miles up Blewett Pass offers a wonderful selection of farm-fresh produce. We particularly enjoy their organically grown d'Anjou pears for their beauty and superb taste. You can pick up some farm fresh eggs from their chickens as well."
– Mountain Home Lodge Chef de Cuisine Kathy Schmidt

> **WINE PAIRING SUGGESTIONS:**
> *Icicle Ridge Winery Ice Riesling*

Prep time: 50 minutes
Chill time: 1 hour
Cook time: 1 hour 10 minutes
Serves: 8-10

Tart Crust
- 3 egg yolks (farm fresh eggs recommended)
- 1/3 cup granulated sugar
- 1/2 cup cold butter, cut into 4 pieces (1 stick)
- 1 tablespoon pure vanilla
- 1-1/2 cups all-purpose flour

Filling
- 12 tablespoons butter (1-1/2 sticks)
- 2 eggs (farm fresh eggs recommended)
- 1/2 cup plus 1 tablespoon granulated sugar
- 3 tablespoons sifted all purpose flour
- 6 cups cold water
- 2 tablespoons fresh squeezed lemon juice
- 4 small or 2 large ripe pears
  (organically grown Nicholson's D'anjou or Bartlett recommended)

Glaze
- 1/2 cup apricot preserves
- 1 tablespoon Asian Pear wine or apple juice (Icicle Ridge Asian Pear Wine recommended)
- 1/4 cup powdered sugar

Tart Crust
Put the egg yolks, sugar, butter and vanilla in the bowl of a food processor. Pulse for 1-2 seconds, 10-12 times. It does not need to be smooth, only lightly blended. Add the flour and pulse quickly until just blended, but NOT smooth.

continued on page 98

ORCHARD PEAR TART (CONTINUED)

continued from page 96

Remove from bowl and gently knead on lightly floured parchment by hand 2-3 times, just until it sticks together. Do not overwork or melt the butter. Gently roll on the parchment to fit a 10 inch tart pan. Transfer shell to pan on the parchment paper. Cover with plastic and chill for about 1 hour.

Filling

To create the custard filling, melt butter in a small saucepan over medium heat until light brown, about 5-6 minutes. Remove from heat and let cool for 5 minutes.

Meanwhile, whisk eggs with sugar in a medium bowl. Whisk in the sifted flour until blended. Add the melted butter, including the brown bits clinging to the pan. Set aside.

Preheat the oven to 375°F. Prepare a large bowl of cold water mixed with lemon juice. Peel the pears using a sharp paring knife. Cut each pear in half lengthwise, remove the core and seeds and place each immediately in the lemon water to avoid discoloration. When done with the pears, gently remove each from the water and let them dry on paper towels.

Cut each pear half into 1/8 inch slices. Slide a narrow spatula under each pear half and transfer to the pastry-lined tart pan, fanning the slices from the center toward the edges. The final pear center may need to be trimmed to fit.

Pour the prepared custard filling in the empty spaces around the pears, but not on top of the fruit. The custard should only come about halfway up the side of the tart.

Bake in the center of the oven for 20 minutes. Reduce heat to 350°F and bake until the custard looks fully cooked and doesn't jiggle, about 40-50 minutes longer. Remove tart from oven and cool completely in pan on rack.

Glaze

To create the glaze, heat the preserves in a small saucepan over low heat until melted. Strain to remove pieces of fruit, if any. Stir in pear wine. Brush pears in the cooled tart with a thin coat of this glaze. Finish tart presentation with a light layer of sifted powdered sugar.

<u>Recipe Tips</u>

- *Serve the tart with a scoop of vanilla bean ice cream and warm caramel sauce (see recipe on page 91) for a delicious dessert.*
- *Prey's Fruit Barn in Leavenworth carries a wonderful selection of jams and preserves for the glaze.*

Salted Caramel Chocolate Mousse Cheesecake

Contributed by Tami Tonge, Baren Haus Restaurant, page 107.

Prep Time: 30 minutes
Cook Time: 2 hours
Chill time: 4 hours to overnight
Serves 12

Wine Pairing Suggestions:
Icicle Ridge Winery Chocolate Cherry Passion
Pasek Cellars Arabica Wine
Willow Crest Syrah Port

Crust
- 1-1/2 cups chocolate graham crackers or Oreo cookies, crushed (about half a package)
- 1 tablespoon sugar
- 5 tablespoons butter, melted

Filling
- 1 tablespoon instant espresso granules
- 1 tablespoon water
- 2 8 oz. packages cream cheese, softened
- 8 oz. package mascarpone cheese
- 3/4 cup sugar
- 1 tablespoon vanilla
- 3/4 cup Godiva chocolate cream liqueur
- 3 eggs
- 6 squares Godiva salted caramel milk chocolate

Topping
- 8 oz. package cream cheese, softened
- 1/4 cup sugar
- 1 teaspoon vanilla
- 4 squares Godiva salted caramel milk chocolate
- 8 oz. tub whipped topping, thawed

Garnish
- Godiva chocolate shavings

Preheat oven to 350°F. Place a large pan (that the cheesecake pan will fit into) filled with 1/2 inch water into the oven while it preheats.

Combine chocolate graham cracker or cookie crumbs, sugar and butter in a small bowl. Press into the bottom of a 9 inch spring form pan. Wrap a large piece of foil around the bottom of the pan to keep the cheesecake dry in the water bath in the oven. Place the crust in the freezer while you mix the filling.

continued on page 101

DESSERTS

Salted Caramel Chocolate Mousse Cheesecake (continued)

continued from page 99

Dissolve espresso granules in water and set aside.

In a large bowl, mix 2 packages cream cheese, mascarpone cheese, sugar, vanilla, chocolate liqueur and espresso mixture until creamy. Whisk the eggs separately and add to the cream cheese mixture. Stir just until blended; do not over mix. Microwave 6 squares of Godiva chocolate in microwave-safe bowl for 30-second increments until melted. Stir into filling mixture. Save the last 4 squares of chocolate for the topping.

Remove the crust from the freezer and add the cream cheese mixture. Place the cheesecake into the preheated water bath and bake for 50 to 60 minutes, or until the center is almost set and top is light brown.

Turn off oven and let cheesecake cook in the oven for 1 hour with the door propped open. Remove from oven, run a knife between the cheesecake and the inside of the pan and place on a cooling rack to finish cooling.

For the topping, beat cream cheese, sugar, vanilla, and 4 squares melted Godiva chocolate in a large mixing bowl. Whisk in whipped cream and spread over cheesecake. Chill in refrigerator for at least 4 hours or overnight.

Garnish with Godiva chocolate shavings.

WINE POACHED PEAR SORBET

**Contributed by Bill and Kathy Lynn,
Enchanted River Inn Bed & Breakfast, page 107.**

"In 2006, Bill was helping Warren Moyles, our favorite local wine maker, bottle wine at La Toscana Winery. Warren gave us a huge Mason jar full of cooking wine. To create a special dessert, Bill poached some Star Crimson pears in the wine. Since we serve sorbet each morning to our Bed and Breakfast guests, we pureed the remaining poached pears and a new tradition was born!" - Kathy Lynn

> **WINE TIP:**
> *Sorbets are generally too delicate to pair with red wine.*

Prep time: 20 minutes
Cook time: 25-40 minutes
Serves: 12

- 2 bottles red wine (i.e. Cabernet, Merlot or Cab-Franc)
- 2 tablespoon sugar
- 1 cinnamon stick
- 6 ripe pears, peeled, cored and halved (Star Crimson or Bosc recommended)

In a large pot, pour the wine, stir in sugar and add cinnamon stick. Add pear halves, making sure the wine covers the pears. Simmer on low for 25 minutes, or until a sharp knife slides easily through a pear. Cool. Spoon pears (without liquid) into food processor and process to the consistency of heavy pudding. Pour the pureed pears into freezer bags and freeze flat.

To serve, thaw in microwave for a few minutes, break into semi-frozen chunks and reprocess in food processor until smooth. Serve immediately.

Recipe Tips
- *Serve with a delicate gingersnap cookie.*
- *Try adding 3 tablespoons semi-sweet chocolate sauce during the puree step.*
- *Use a melon baller to scoop sorbet and garnish with mint for a beautiful presentation.*

Wine Soaked Cherries & Pears over Pound Cake

Contributed by Willow Crest Winery, page 14.

Prep time: 20 minutes
Cook time: 20 minutes
Serves: 4

- 1/2 cup red wine (Willow Crest Leavenworth Red recommended)
- 1/2 cup sugar
- Zest of 1/2 lemon
- 3/4 lb. cherries, pitted (about 2 cups)
- 2 pears, peeled and sliced
- 4 thick slices pound cake
- Softened butter to taste
- Whipped cream topping

> **WINE PAIRING SUGGESTIONS:**
> *Cascadia Winery*
> *Sakura Dessert Wine*
> *Pasek Cellars Syrah Port*
> *Willow Crest Winery Syrah Port*

Combine wine, sugar and lemon zest in a medium saucepan over medium-high heat. Stir until the sugar dissolves. Stir in the cherries. Bring to a boil, reduce heat, and simmer for 10 minutes.

Stir in pears and simmer for an additional 5 minutes.

Spread pound cake with butter and toast or broil in the oven with the door open until golden brown.

Generously spoon fruit and juices over cake. Serve warm, topped with a dollop of whipped cream.

Notes

"Getting Some Color" by Kerry Siderius

"Cashmere" by Kerry Siderius

Contributors

Pamela Kiehn, Beecher Hill House

Beecher Hill House was built in the early 1900's as a private residence. The restored inn is perfect for getaways, weddings or other events. Overnight stays include gourmet breakfasts and complimentary wine and hors d'oeuvres. Catering is also available.

9991 Beecher Hill Rd., Peshastin, WA
509.548.0559 or 866.414.0559
beecherhill.com

Tami Tonge, Baren Haus Restaurant

Baren Haus Restaurant is the oldest family-owned restaurant in Leavenworth. Originally started as a pizza and pasta restaurant in 1981, they now also offer German entrées, steak, seafood, and homemade desserts.

208 9th St., Leavenworth, WA
509.548.4535
barenhaus.com

Dave Hambleton, The Cheesemonger's Shop

In 2002, the Dot Com bubble burst and Dave and Barb Hambleton needed jobs and a lifestyle change. They loved the food and people angles of running a bed and breakfast, but prefer that there are no beds to make or bathrooms to clean in a cheese shop. They've had a blast learning the ropes.

819 Front Street, Leavenworth, WA
509.548.9011
cheesemongersshop.com

Bill & Kathy Lynn, Enchanted River Inn

Nature's breathtaking view from the Enchanted River Inn offers guests the beauty of the Wenatchee River and Cascade Mountains. Suites at the Inn are designed for your special occasion or romantic getaway, complete with delicious and unique gourmet breakfasts.

9700 E. Leavenworth Rd., Leavenworth, WA
509.548.9797
enchantedriverinn.com

Contributors (Continued)

Reed Carlson, Icicle Valley Photography

Reed Carlson operates a full-service photography studio in Leavenworth, specializing in weddings, portraiture, commercial and documentary projects.

509.548.0606
reed@iciclevalleyphotography.com
iciclevalleyphotography.com

4119 E. Madison,
Seattle, WA
206.324.0432
jrleagueseattle.org

The Junior League of Seattle

Simply Classic, published by the Seattle Junior League, is a bestselling Northwest cookbook and winner of the Tabasco Award. Profits from cookbook sales support Junior League projects and training programs.

Kasey Koski, Artist, Designer and Domestic Adventurer

Kasey Koski's talents range from urban gardener to mixed media artist to domestic adventurer. Any task that could be improved by a touch of creativity – graphic design, painting, knitting, cobbling shoes – might turn into her next project.

kaseykoski@yahoo.com.

Kerry Siderius, Watercolor Artist

Kerry is an apple orchardist's daughter from Bridgeport, WA. Their farm sat along the banks of the Columbia, where Canada geese, salmon and apples were plentiful. She began painting her surroundings at three years old and she's never stopped.

Gallery: Rio Vista Wines
24415 Hwy 97, Chelan, WA
kerry@kerrysiderius.com
kerrysiderius.com

Contributors (Continued)

Joanne Saliby, *Living Well* blog author

Joanne Saliby is the author of the Wenatchee World *Living Well* blog. Having lived in Leavenworth since the inception of the local wine industry, she has become acquainted with nearly all local wines. Joanne does food and wine pairings for the Wenatchee Enological Society and several local wineries.

jasaliby@aol.com

Marissa Maharaj Photography

Marissa Maharaj is a wedding and lifestyle photographer in the Seattle area. Her work is fresh, modern and playful, with authentic storytelling at the heart of all her images.

206.604.5372
marissamaharaj@gmail.com
marissamaharaj.com

Executive Chef Thomas Obregon & Chef de Cuisine Kathy Schmidt, Mountain Home Lodge

Leavenworth's premier resort offers gourmet dinners with advance reservation April - November, snow dependent. Winter reserved for overnight lodging guests only. Menus feature the highest quality local ingredients whenever possible.

8201 Mountain Home Rd., Leavenworth, WA
800.414.2378 or 509.548.7077
mthome.com

Taelor Feinberg, The Oil and Vinegar Cellar

International travel, fine dining experience and early lessons in her mother's kitchen inspired Taelor's passion for food and people.

633 Front St., Ste. F, Leavenworth, WA
509.470.7684

CONTRIBUTORS (CONTINUED)

Marlies Egberding, The Savory Table Catering

Marlies Egberding enjoys creating dishes using the dessert and fruit wines made by her friends at Pasek Cellars.

thesavorytable@gmail.com

South Restaurant

South owners Cappy Bond and Price Gledhill pride themselves on using only the highest quality ingredients and making all their food from scratch. They have a full bar, with more than 50 tequilas and five beers on tap.

913 Front St., Leavenworth, WA
509.888.HEAT
southleavenworth.com

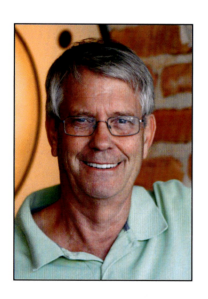

Richard Uhlhorn, Photographer

Richard Uhlhorn has been a professional photographer and journalist in the Lake Chelan Valley since 1988. He has enjoyed the new adventure in food photography that *Savoring Chelan* and *Savoring Leavenworth* have provided.

509.682.0602
richard@richarduhlhorn.com
richarduhlhorn.com.

Executive Chef Daniel Carr & Chef du Cuisine Steve Coin, Visconti's Ristorante Italiano

Visconti's restaurants feature award-winning local and Italian wine selections. Add gourmet Italian cuisine and you have a recipe for a great dining experience.
viscontis.com

Visconti's - Leavenworth
636 Front St., Leavenworth, WA
509.548.1213

Visconti's - Wenatchee
1737 N. Wenatchee Ave., Wenatchee, WA
509.662.5013

"Grapes Over the Columbia" by Kerry Siderius

INDEX ~ CONTRIBUTORS

Photography and Design

Carlson, Reed .... 5, 6, 13, 20, 24 (background), **108**
Koski, Kasey .... Cover, page and logo design, **108**
  Background photos: 23, 26-28, 31-34, 38, 40-44, 47-50, 52-53, 55-57, 59-62, 65-68, 71-73, 75, 78-86, 91, 93, 104
Maharaj, Marissa 16, **109**
Uhlhorn, Richard .... back cover photo, **110**
  .... 7, 9, 10, 11, 15, 17, 18, 19, 120
  Full page color recipe photos: 25, 30, 39, 51, 58, 63, 64, 69, 70, 74, 77, 97, 100 Background photos: 29, 37, 54, 76, 89, 90, 92, 94, 95, 96, 98, 99, 101, 102, 103

Recipe Contributors

Bond, Cappy 31, 68, **110**
Carr, Daniel 38, 50, 57, 65, **110**
Coin, Steve 38, 50, 57, 65, **110**
Egberding, Marlies 32, 78, 95, **110**
Egner, Candace 5, 67
Feinberg, Taelor 26, 49, **109**
Fraser, Morgan 89, 90, **120**
Gledhill, Price 31, 68, **110**
Hambleton, Dave 40, 54, 61, 72, **107**
Hartmann, Traci 6, 82, 83
Junior League 29, **108**
Kiehn, Pamela 24, 62, 71, 75, **107**
Lynn, Bill 102, **107**
Lynn, Kathy 102, **107**
Mitrakul, Danielle 9, 84
Moyles, Julie 13, 29, 42, 44, 79, 86, 93, 94
Newsom, Rob 7, 43, 76, 80
Obregon, Thomas 96, **109**
Saliby, Joanne 41, 53, 60, 73, **109**
Schmidt, Kathy 27, **109**
Siderius, Kerry 48, **108**
Stemilt Creek Winery 17, 33
Tonge, Tami 99, **107**
Willow Crest Winery 14, 103
Wood, Kristen 12, 23, 37, 47, 55, 56, 66, 92
Yanagimachi, Alan 8, 81, 91

Watercolor Paintings

Siderius, Kerry .... Cover paintings, **108**
  .... 3, 4, 21, 22, 35, 36, 45, 46, 87, 88, 105, 106, 108, 111

***Bold page numbers** denote the information page about the contributor and include their contact information.*

112 SAVORING LEAVENWORTH

INDEX ~ RECIPES BY NAME

Apple Pecan Brie	23
Apple Sweet Potato Roast Pork	47
Artist's Vacation Greek Lamb	48
Audrey's Apple Pie	89
Audrey's Pie Crust	90
Balsamic Glazed Salmon	49
Beecher Hill Roasted Grapes	24
Beet Salad	38
Bleu Cheese Pear Salad	37
Butternut Squash Ravioli with Sage Butter	50
Caramel Sauce with Apple Wine	91
Chorizo Yam Bisque	40
Creamy Smoked Salmon & Asparagus	53
Dave's Mac & Cheese	54
Feta Mint Lamb Burgers	55
Flank Steak Portabella Sandwiches	56
Gazpacho Blanco	41
Gnocchi with Roasted Tomato & Red Pepper Sauce	57
Gorgonzola Balsamic Fruit Plate	26
Grandma Judy's Sour Cream Pear Pie	92
Grilled Ahi Tuna Salad	42
Grilled Lamb Burgers in Red Wine	60
Gumbo	43
Hambleton Hominy Casserole	61
Herb's Sweet & Tangy Salmon Sauce	62
La Toscana Apple Coffee Cake	93
Lemon Crab Linguini	65
Lobster Mac & Cheese	66
Mango Raspberry Cobbler	94
Mediterranean Rack of Lamb	67
Mole de Oaxaca	68
Mushroom Artichoke Chicken	71
Mushroom Risotto	72
Mushroom, Tomme & Roasted Tomato Crostini	27

INDEX ~ RECIPES BY NAME (CONTINUED)

Orchard Pear Tart 96
Perfectly Pesto Cheesecake 29
Raspberry Cheesecake Sauce 95
Red Wine Cherry Pork 73
Roast Pork Loin with Bartlett Pear Sauce 75
Saffron Quail 76
Salmon in Balsamic Blackberry Wine Sauce 78
Salsa Verde 31
Salted Caramel Chocolate Mousse Cheesecake 99
Scalloped Oysters 79
Shrimp Etouffee 80
Spaghetti with Merlot Tomato Sauce 81
Sweet & Savory Pineapple Salsa 32
Sweet & Spicy Black Beans 82
Tarragon and Crab Stuffed Tomatoes 44
Thai Cashew Chicken 83
Thai Coconut Bouillabaisse 84
Tuscan Cabbage and Mushrooms 86
Walnut Crusted Brie with Apple Cherry Chutney 33
Wine Poached Pear Sorbet 102
Wine Soaked Cherries & Pears Over Pound Cake 103

INDEX ~ WINES BY WINERY (CONTINUED)

'37 Cellars 5
    Cabernet Sauvignon 48
    Columbia Valley Chardonnay 42, 53
    Pepper Bridge Merlot 67, 68

Bella Terrazza Vineyards 6
    Estate Bella Rosso 72
    Estate Cabernet Franc 73
    Estate Chardonnay 79
    Estate Gewürztraminer 83
    Estate Lemberger 60
    Estate Pinot Grigio 82
    Estate Riesling 65, 83

Boudreaux Cellars 7
    Cabernet Sauvignon 48
    Chardonnay 43, 53, 66, 80
    Frangio: Sangiovese/Cabernet Franc Red Blend 27
    Riesling 75, 80, 83
    Syrah 40, 76
    Reserve Cabernet Sauvignon 76

Cascadia Winery 8
    Apple Wine 33, 75
    Merlot 81
    Roussanne 24, 31
    Sakura Dessert Wine 103

Crayelle Cellars 9
    Dry Riesling 42, 43, 65, 84
    Syrah 67

Eagle Creek Winery 10
    Adler Weiss 40
    Gewürztraminer 80
    White Riesling 41, 47
    Cabernet Sauvignon 54
    Chardonnay 50

INDEX ~ WINES BY WINERY (CONTINUED)

    Merlot 68
    Syrah 40

Horan Estates 11
    Cabernet Sauvignon 60
    HVH Red Blend 73

Icicle Ridge Winery 12
    The Blondes Gewürztraminer 37
    Chardonnay 79
    Chocolate Cherry Passion 99
    Ice Riesling 23, 92, 96
    Merlot 55
    Romanze Blend 55
    Sauvignon Blanc 66
    Syrah 56

La Toscana Winery 13
    Annika's Riesling 29, 93
    Cabernet Sauvignon/Cabernet Franc 72
    Lemberger 86
    Rosso Toscano 72, 81
    Ellie Kay's Sangiovese 27, 57

Pasek Cellars 14
    Arabica Wine 99
    Blackberry Dessert Wine 23
    Chardonnay 54
    Muscat Canelli 26, 95
    Pineapple Wine 32
    Raspberry Dessert Wine 94, 95
    Syrah Port 103

Ryan Patrick Vineyards 15
    Naked Chardonnay 44, 71
    Reserve Chardonnay 38, 50, 53, 65
    Rock Island Red 27
    Rosé 38, 49

INDEX ~ WINES BY WINERY (CONTINUED)

Silvara Vineyards **16**
    60/40 Red Blend 60
    Chardonnay 50, 66
    Malbec 48
    Pinot Grigio 29, 43
    Riesling 75
    Syrah 56

Stemilt Creek Winery **17**
    Estate Syrah 56, 67
    Sweet Adelaide White Blend 31, 33

Swakane Winery & Tasting Room **18**
    Estate Late Harvest Riesling 89, 92
    Estate Rosé of Cabernet Franc 38

Waterville Winery **19**
    Gewürztraminer 62
    NOaked Chardonnay 79, 82
    Riesling 71
    Temperanillo 86

Wedge Mountain Winery **20**
    Chardonnay 86
    Lemberger (Dry) 47
    Dry Riesling 41, 84
    Lemberger (Semi-Sweet) 61, 73, 78
    Pinot Grigio 44
    Roses & Rubies 94, 95
    Trois Chevaux Rouges Red Blend 57, 61

Willow Crest Winery **14**
    Syrah Port 99, 103
    Riesling 62, 82

Washington Fruit Harvest Dates

Apples	May	June	July	Aug.	Sept.	Oct.
Braeburn						X
Fuji					X	X
Gala				X	X	
Gingergold				X		
Golden Delicious					X	X
Granny Smith						X
Honey Crisp					X	
Jonagold					X	X
Pink Lady						X
Red Delicious					X	X

Berries	May	June	July	Aug.	Sept.	Oct.
Blackberries		X	X	X		
Blueberries		X	X			
Raspberries		X	X	X		

Cherries	May	June	July	Aug.	Sept.	Oct.
Bing	X	X				
Chelan		X	X			
Lapin		X	X			
Montmorency		X				
Rainier	X	X				
Sweetheart		X	X			

Peaches	May	June	July	Aug.	Sept.	Oct.
Cresthaven				X	X	
Donut			X	X		
Elberta					X	
O'Henry				X	X	
Red Globe				X	X	
Red Haven				X		

Pears	May	June	July	Aug.	Sept.	Oct.
Asian					X	
Bartlett				X	X	
Bosc					X	
D'Anjou					X	

Other Fruits	May	June	July	Aug.	Sept.	Oct.
Apricots			X			
Nectarines			X	X		
Plumcots			X	X		

Note: Harvest varies yearly based on weather; these are estimates only.

Acknowledgements

Savoring Leavenworth is a collaboration, and I would like to thank everyone who made this book possible.

Thank you first and foremost to Alex and Joanne Saliby, for putting in hours of effort to make sure the wine pairings were the best fit possible for each and every dish.

Thank you to Pat Rutledge at A Book for All Seasons in Leavenworth for being supportive of my project - and local writers in general - and helping me to implement all the pieces to the very best of my ability.

Thank you to Reed Carlson for doing such a great job getting the last minute pictures I needed.

Thank you to my recipe testers and tasters, who gave me great feedback, made sure the recipes were as good as they could be and many times let me invade their kitchens: Angela Berg, Dan Erwin, Kim and Lucas Green, Kim Hildenbrand, Anna Koenig, Kasey Koski, Mariah Luft, Eric and Christina Merhar, Rose Weagant Norton, Candice and Ralph Reed, Molly Steere, and the "Sauce Kings" Zeb Postelwait, Thad Brewer and Steve Misenheimer.

Thank you to Jesse Howard for his insights on the Leavenworth area and for being a master at sauce improvement strategies. Thank you to Kate Koenig for letting me take over her kitchen and her dinner menus to start off the testing process, and suggesting restaurants to approach.

Thank you to the Wenatchee Women's Writers Group for their support and feedback: Yvette Davis, Anita Van Stralen, Haley Whitehall, Jen Morrison and especially Nancy Trucano, who valiantly made it through the first draft before any corrections had been made.

Thank you to Terri Weagant for recipe and taste testing, and for existential conversations during the first round of recipe corrections.

Thank you to Roni Freund for completing the final edit and therefore giving me peace of mind.

Thank you to all the 30+ recipe contributors and wineries; the book would not exist without you.

Thank you especially to the crew from *Savoring Chelan* who stuck with me to make yet another project better than I could have done it alone: graphic artist Kasey Koski, photographer Richard Uhlhorn and watercolor artist Kerry Siderius.

And last but not least, thank you to my parents Janet and Stu for continuing to support me in all that I do.

About the Author

Photo by Richard Uhlhorn

Morgan Fraser is a Chelan Valley native whose travel addiction has taken her all over the world in search of new adventures, foods and flavors to pair with wine.

Morgan attended Manson High School and grew up on an apple orchard, where she learned to differentiate between the taste of store-bought off-season apples and the unmistakable flavor of fresh-picked fruit. She still considers herself an apple aficionado.

Morgan attended Washington State University and studied abroad for a year in Spain, where her love for travel – and wine – began to develop. After graduating with degrees in journalism and Spanish, she lived, traveled and worked in many countries and several states.

The success of Morgan's first book, *Savoring Chelan: Pairing Local Wine with Regional Recipes,* led her to create *Savoring Leavenworth.* The books have taught her a lot about writing, publishing, recipe testing and the importance of cleaning while you cook. She now spends her time writing fiction, non-fiction and travelogues and creating new fusion dishes that pair spice with nearly everything.

You can read more about Morgan's culinary concoctions and adventures at savoringchelan.com/blog.html.